Tourism Service English

관광서비스영어

Wan-Hyung Lee

BAEKSAN Publishing Co

머리말

관광사업은 우리 국가경제의 一翼을 담당하고 있으며, 국가적인 산업으로 육성해 나가야 할 과제를 안고 있다.

觀光서비스業務의 흐름은 意思疏通에 기초를 두고 있으며, 國際共通語인 英語를 매체로 한 觀光實務 英語會話를 익히고자 하는 專門人 養成과 해외여행을 즐기고자 하는 일반인을 위해, 특히 다음 사항에 力點을 주어 집필하였다.

1. 觀光案內員 또는 觀光實務 從事者들에게 필요한 出入國 手續 및 航空서비스 實務英語
2. 觀光호텔서비스에 적응할 英語會話
3. 觀光通譯案內員 및 國外旅行案內員用 英語會話
4. 觀光 專門人이나 國內外 모든 여행자에게 적용되는 狀況別 英語會話
5. 通譯案內員으로써 반드시 알아두어야 할 國內 有名 觀光地 등에 관한 案內英語의 實例
6. 就業·海外留學 및 通譯案內員에 대비한 Interview英語, 英文履歷書, 應試願書 請求文, 호텔종사원 및 通譯案內員試驗에 대비한 豫想問題
7. 筆者가 講義 및 通譯案內員試驗委員 등 一線 現場經驗에서 얻은 英語 하나하나의 表現·技法 등 例文을 들고, 脚註를 달아 스스로 학습하는 이에게 便益을 주었다.

아무쪼록 國內外 觀光案內員은 물론, 觀光 業體에 종사하고자 하는 學徒 및 해외 여행을 하는 일반인들의 좋은 반려가 되길 바라는 마음 간절하다.

著 者 識

修訂 增補版을 내면서

제24회 Seoul Olympiad를 起點으로 2002 FIFA World Cup, Kyongju World Culture Expo, PATA 개최 등 韓國觀光의 새로운 轉換期를 맞이하였으며, 挑戰과 變化(Challenge and Change)의 情報化時代에 걸맞게 긍정적인 자세로 한국관광산업을 선진국으로 유도하고 있는 現時點에서 관광인의 責任이 막중하다고 할 수 있다.

이런 긍지와 자부심을 가지고, 國際化·地球村化라는 時代的 潮流에 便乘되어 各 部門에서 脫 冷戰 現象과 東西陣營의 화해분위기는 世界平和와 繁榮의 길로 향하는 활기찬 觀光國으로 이끌어가는 것이 우리의 觀光人의 자세, 義務와 責任이라고 할 수 있다.

筆者가 本書를 出刊 후 하와이대학(U. H.)에서 客員敎授로 근무하면서, 그리고 Florida와 California 등의 Seminar와 Session 등을 통해 觀光과 現地 住民의 觀光認知 등에 관한 硏究體驗을 통해 습득한 것들을 기존의 原稿에 修訂 增補를 거듭하면서 微力이나마 韓國觀光에 헌신해 왔다. 觀光學徒와 有關業種에 종사하는 분들의 呼應에 보답하고자 새로운 覺悟로 修訂 增補版을 내게 되었다. 江湖 諸位의 끊임없는 指導와 鞭撻을 바라마지 않는다.

Basic human encounter is one of the supreme experiences of life. Tourism has the potential to give that encounter to increased numbers of people. Across the boundaries of nationality and of wealth it should bo possible for people to recognize that they belong to one another and are part of a single human family. When tourism realizes its potential for creating that unity, world peace may not be an impossible dream.

"We travel to learn; and I have never been in a country where they did not do something better than we do it, think some thoughts better than we think, catch some inspiration from heights above our own."

2003年 新春 退村 愚居에서

李 完 炯

C/O/N/T/E/N/T/S

PART I AIRLINE SERVICE

PART II HOTEL SERVICE

PART III TOUR GUIDE

PART IV OVERSEAS TOUR CONDUCTOR SERVICE

PART V SITUATIONAL DIALOGS

PART VI GUIDE ENGLISH ABOUT KOREA

PART VII INTERVIEW ENGLISH

APPENDIX

PART 1

AIRLINE SERVICE

Unit 1 RESERVATION

▪A = Reservation Clerk, ▪B = Passenger

Dialog 1

A : Korean Air Lines. May I help you, sir?
B : I'd like to fly to Pusan on Saturday, the 3rd.
A : Yes, sir. What time would you like to fly?
B : I'd like to leave around 11:30 in the morning.
A : May I have your name, please?
B : Thomas Smith.

Dialog 2

A : Thank you, Mr. Smith. I can make a reservation for you on Flight 201 which leaves 11:30.
B : That's fine. I'll take that one.
A : May I have your phone number, please?
B : 312-1234.
A : Thanks a lot. You can purchase your ticket at one of our ticket offices.
B : Okay, I'll do that. Good-bye.
A : Thanks for calling.

reservation : 예약. Ex. I'd like to make a reservation.
passenger : 승객.
flight 201 : 201호기 편.
a lot = very much.
purchase : 구매하다.
Thanks for calling. : 전화 주셔서 감사합니다.
Thanks a lot : P.48 참조.

Dialog 3

A : Japan Air Lines, Miss Kim speaking. May I help you, sir?

B : Yes, I'd like to get a seat to New York tomorrow.

A : What time would you like to make it? We have two flights at 11 AM, and 2 p.m.

B : I'd like to fly at 11 a.m.

A : First class or economy class, sir?

B : First class, please.

A : May I have your name and phone number, please?

B : Lyn Martin. 312-4321.

Useful Expressions

1. Korean Air Lines. May I help you, sir?
   Japan Air Lines.
   Domestic Reservations.
   International Reservations.

2. Yes, I'd like to fly to New York
   get a seat to Tokyo.

This is Miss Kim speaking : 미스 김입니다.(전화로)
flight : 비행편
AM : 오전, PM : 오후
economy class : 이등석(second class란 말을 쓰지 않도록).
first class : 일등석
cut-rate : 할인가격(미식)
cut-price : (영식)

fly to Hong Kong.
make a reservation.

3. You may purchase your ticket at
any KAL office.
any travel agency
one of KAL offices.

4. Your reservation number is 205.
312.
114.

5. Shall I make a reservation for you ?
put you on the waiting list ?
have him call you back ?

That's all right is a frequent response to an apology.
Ex. I'm sorry, I broke your mirror.
/That's all right.
That's right frequently means 아! 그런가?
Ex. I won't be here tomorrow.
/That's right. You're going to New York, aren't you?
ticketing : 발권

Unit 2 TICKETING

■A = Ticket Agent, ■B = Passenger

Dialog 1

A : Good morning. May I help you, sir?

B : Yes, I want to go to Tokyo on May 1st. Would you give me a ticket, please?

A : First class or economy class, sir?

B : First class, please.

A : We have one at 11:30.

B : I'd like to take that one.

Dialog 2

A : Would you like a round-trip ticket?

B : No, just one-way.

A : May I see your travel documents, please?

B : Here you are.

A : Thank you for waiting, sir. Your ticket for Tokyo, first class, on Flight 502 leaving 11:30 on May 1st. The fare is 329 dollars, sir.

B : Here you are.

round-trip ticket : 왕복 승차권(미식), return ticket (영식)
one-way ticket : 편도 승차권(미식), single ticket(영식)
travel documents : 여행서류
fare : 요금(교통), 호텔의 객실료는 'room rate'라고 한다.

Dialog 3

A : Good afternoon. May I help you, sir?

B : I want to get a ticket for Chicago.

A : Did you make a reservation, sir?

B : No, I didn't.

A : When would you like to leave?

B : On October 25th.

A : We have two flights available at 10 p.m. and 6:30 p.m. Which one would you prefer, sir?

B : I want to take 6:30 p.m. flight. Economy class, please.

Useful Expressions

1. Would you like a one-way ticket?
   a round trip ticket.
   a first class.
   an economy class.

2. Have a good flight.
   a pleasant trip.
   a nice day.

available : 이용할 수 있는. **e.g. ; room available, seat available**
prefer : 더 좋아하다. *Ex. I prefer apples to pears.*

3. Thank you for waiting.
calling.
listening to.

4. I'd like to go to New York.
Hong Kong.
Tokyo.

5. Would you like to purchase your ticket now?
get
buy

6. Do you have any seat preferences, ma'am?

7. Could you put me in the non-smoking section?

Unit 3 CHECKING-IN (I)

■A = Agent, ■B = Passenger

Dialog 1

A : Good morning. May I help you, sir?

B : Yes, I'm going to take your flight 205 for Cheju.

A : May I have your ticket, please?

B : Here you are.

A : Do you have any baggage to check?

B : Yes, I have one suitcase here.

A : May we have it on the scale, please? Which seat would you prefer, sir?

B : I think I will take a window seat.

Dialog 2

A : Good evening. May I help you, sir?

B : Yes, I'd like to check in, please.

A : May I see your passport and ticket, please?

baggage : 수화물, 짐.
airport service charge : 공항세(a.s.c.)
boarding pass : 탑승권.

- **C. I. Q.** : 출입국 절차를 통틀어 흔히 'Government Formalities'라고 하는데, 그 순서는
  ① Quarantine Officer(검역관)에게 vaccination certificate(예방주사 접종 증명서-색깔이 노랗기 때문에 흔히 'yellow card'라고 함)를 보인다.

B : Here you are.

A : Would you put your baggage on the scale, please? I must collect W3,000 for the airport service charge.

B : Okay, here you are.

A : Your ticket, passport ana boarding pass. Have a nice flight, sir.

B : Thanks a lot.

Dialog 3

B : I'd like to check in, please.

A : May I see your ticket and passport, please?

B : Ok, here you are.

A : You're going to New York on Flight 507, economy class, aren't you?

B : Right.

A : Your seat is 7A, sir.

B : Where do I go now?

A : Would you please go to Customs and Immigration?

B : Thanks a lot.

A : Have a nice flight.

② Immigration(출입국 관리) card를 제출하여 여권의 점검을 받고 점검이 끝나면 stamp를 찍고 출·입국 연월일(date of departure, date of arrival)을 기입해 줌으로써 두번째 절차가 끝난다.

③ Customs Inspector(세관 검사원)에게 휴대품의 검사를 받는다. 출국시는 고급 시계, 카메라 등 귀중품은 휴대 출국 증명서 수속으로 여권에 기재, 승인, 날인을 받아 간수해 두어야 귀국시 재 반입 확인을 얻어 과세 대상이 되지 않는다.

Useful Expressions

1. May I see your ticket and passport, please?
   Can
   Could

2. Would you put your baggage on the scale?
   Would you mind putting
   Please put

3. Your seat number is 26A.
   17C.

4. This is your boarding pass.
   baggage claim tag.

5. The flight will leave at 10 o'clock.

6. Is the plane on time?
   Is the plane on schedule?

baggage claim tag : 소하물예치증 ; 짐표

- **Check-In**

Airport하면 국제공항(international airport)과 국내 여행자를 위한 domestic airport가 있다. Ticket counter는 어느 공항이든 자기가 타고 갈 비행기 회사의 이름을 기억해서 해당 counter에게 비행기표, 여권, 예방주사 접종증명서를 제출한다. 여기서 짐은 제한 중량 초과여부를 확인하고 좌석으로 가지고 갈 hand baggage를 제외하고는 예치증(baggage claim tag)을 항공권의 표지에 붙인다. 제출된 여권 등과 함께 탑승권(boarding pass)이 인도된다. 국내 여행의 경우는 여기서 check-in 수속이 끝나고 국외 여행의 경우 출국카드(embarkation card)가 나오므로 여기에 기록할 사항을 적어 넣으면(fill in the form) 역시 수속이 끝나, boarding announce만을 기다리면 된다.

Unit 4 CHECKING-IN (II)

■A = Agent, ■B = Passenger

Dialog 1

A : Good morning. May I help you, sir?

B : Yes, I want to check in.

A : May I have your name, please?

B : Thomas Brown.

A : Yes, we have your reservation. May I have your ticket?

B : Here you are.

Dialog 2

A : May I ask you for the airport tax?

B : How much is it?

A : Three dollars and 30 cents, please.

B : Here you are.

A : Thank you.

airport tax : 공항세(공식 명칭은 airport service charge : a.s.c.)
extra weight : 초과중량.
lobby : 로비. 복도.
upstairs : 위층.
downstairs : 아래층
departure lounge : 탑승객 대합실.

Dialog 3

A : May I weigh your baggage? Are you going to pay for the extra weight?

B : Of course.

A : Here's your baggage claim tag.

B : How can I get to the departure lounge?

A : You'll find the escalator at the end. The departure lounge is on the second floor.

Useful Expressions

1. Would you like a seat in the smoking section?
   the non-smoking section ?
   the middle ?

2. Is the non-smoking section all right with you?

3. I'm sorry, sir. I have no more window seats in the smoking section.

4. Is there an aisle seat available?

5. Please go upstairs.
   downstairs.
   to the 2nd floor.

departure information counter : 출국 안내계(카운터)

6. Do you have anything to declare?
any baggage to check?
anything to eat?

7. I'm going to take your flight 207.
check in.
weigh your baggage.

8. May I go now ?
have your ticket?

9. Please show me where the departure information counter is.

10. Are there duty-free shops in the departure lounge?

- 게이트에서 직접 비행기를 탈 경우와 공항버스를 이용할 경우가 있다.
- 입구에서 스튜어디스에게 「탑승카드」를 보이고 좌석으로 안내 받는다. 국내선 등에서 좌석 지정이 없을 때에는 선착순으로 자기 마음에 드는 자리에 앉지만, 예약(Occupied : Reserved)의 표시가 있는 좌석에는 앉을 수 없다.
- 머리 위의 시렁에는 코트 같은 가벼운 것을 얹고 가방 같은 것은 좌석 밑에 넣는 것이 보통이다. 둘 장소가 없을 때에는 스튜어디스에게 (Will you keep this for me?)라고 말하여 맡기도록 한다.
- 만년필이나 향수병은 기내의 기압 때문에 속 내용물이 새는 수가 있으므로 비닐봉지 등에 넣어 두는 것이 좋다.

duty-free shop : 면세품 상점.
export(import) duties : 수출(수입)세.
go aboard the plane : 탑승하다.

Unit 5 GOING ABOARD THE PLANE

■A = Stewardess, ■B = Passenger

Dialog 1

A : Your boarding pass, please!
B : Here, it is.
A : Thank you.
B : Where's my seat?
A : 25A. Just over there, sir.

Dialog 2

A : Good evening. May I help you, sir?
B : Miss, where can I put my bag?
A : You can put your coat and small things on the rack over your head. And your bag here at your feet.
B : I have two bags. I'm afraid I can't put these two bags down here. Can I put one on the rack?
A : All right, sir.

Dialog 3

A : May I help you, sir?
B : Where's the rest room?

A : Behind that curtain.

B : Excuse me, but will you please watch my suitcases for a minute?

A : Yes, I will.

B : Thank you again.

A : You're welcome.

Useful Expressions

1. Where can I put my bag?

2. You can put it on the rack.

3. I'm afraid I can't go with you.

4. I'm afraid I can't understand what you say.

5. Your seat numbers are 4A, 4B, and 4C.

6. Please show me how to use this seat belt.

7. **A** : Excuse me. Would you mind trading seats with me?
   B : Not at all. I prefer a window seat.

- **trade seats** (자리를 바꿔 앉다)에서나 **change trains** (기차를 갈아타다), **shake hands**(악수하다) 등에서 복수 's'가 필연적으로 붙는 것을 기억하자.
- 이륙한다는 방송이 들리고, 「Fasten seat belt(벨트착용)」의 사인이 나오면 좌석벨트를 멘다. 「No smoking(금연)」의 사인이 나와 있는 동안에는 담배를 피우지 않도록 한다.
- 좌석에는 등을 조절하는 버튼(Seat Reclining Button) · 재떨이 · 음악방송을 듣기 위한 채널 버튼(Music Selection Switch) 등이 달려있다. 기내에서 편히 앉아 즐기기 위해서는 이런 설비를 잘 이용하는 것도 필요하다. 여행 도중에는 피로하지 않도록 하는 것이 아주 중요하다.

Unit 6 TAKING-OFF

■A = Stewardess, ■B = Passenger

Dialog 1

A : I'm sorry, sir, but you are not allowed to smoke till the "No Smoking" lamp over there goes out.

B : Oh, forgive me, I didn't notice it. By the way, would you please tell me how to fasten my seat belt?

A : Certainly, sir. Just insert this part of the belt into this clasp.

B : Oh. I see.

Dialog 2

A : I think it's a bit too tight. You'd better loosen it a little bit.

B : I will. Um, I feel much more comfortable now. Stewardess, will you give me some pills for airsickness? I'm afraid I might get sick.

take off : 이륙하다.
be allowed to : ~가 허용되다.
insert : 삽입하다.
clasp : 고리, 걸쇠.
fasten seat belt : 좌대를 매다.
by the way,… : 그건 그렇고(화제를 바꿀 때 사용되는 표현). 화제를 바꿀 때에 'not to change the subject, but…' 또는 'to change the subject, …'라는 고상한 표현이 있다.
air sickness : 비행기 멀미.
high sickness : 고공병.
sea sickness : 배 멀미.

A : I'll bring you some in a moment, but please don't be nervous. Travelling by jetliners is very comfortable these days. Planes today have hardly any vibration unless the weather is exceptionally bad.

Dialog 3

A : The "Fasten Seat Belt" and "No Smoking" signs are out.

B : Now we can relax. I didn't know that jetliners were so comfortable.

A : Neither did I. Care for a cigarette?

B : Yes, thank you.

Useful Expressions

1. Do you care for a cigarette?
2. Do you care for some candy?
3. Push the button just above your head.
4. You are not allowed to smoke.
5. Smoking is not allowed here.
6. Please fasten your seat belt and put out your cigarette until after we take off.
7. Because of the bad weather conditions, we have to wait a little while.
8. Can I use the P.A. system? (P.A. : public address).

Unit 7 FOOD AND BEVERAGE SERVICE

▪A = Stewardess, ▪B = Passenger

Dialog 1

A : What would you like to drink, sir?

B : What do you have?

A : We have coffee, tea, orange juice......

B : Orange juice, please.

Dialog 2

A : Which would you like, sir? We have chicken and beef.

B : I think I'll have chicken, please.

A : Yes. sir.

B : Thank you.

Dialog 3

A : Did you call me? What can I do for you, sir?

B : I want some cigarettes. What kinds of cigarettes do you have?

A : We have Kent, Salem, Winston, Marlboro......

B : I want Salem. Two packs, please.

Useful Expressions

1. What would you like to drink?
2. What do you have?
3. We have all kinds of fruit juice.
4. Which would you like? Which do you prefer?
5. What can I do for you?

SMILE

A smile costs nothing but gives much.

It enriches those who give it. It takes but a moment but the memory of it sometimes lasts forever.

None is so rich or mighty that she can get along without it. None is so poor but that she cannot be made richer by it. A smile creates happiness in the home, promotes goodwill in business, and is the cornerstone of friendship.

It can perk up the weary, bring cheer to the discouraged, sunshine to the sad, and nature's best antidote for trouble.

Yet it cannot be bought, begged, borrowed or stolen
for it is something that is of no value to anyone else
it is given away.

When people are too tired to give you a smile,
give them one of yours.

No one needs a smile so much as she who has none to give.

Unit 8 BLANKET AND MOVIE SERVICE

■A = Passenger, ■B = Stewardess

Dialog 1

A : Miss!

B : Yes, sir?

A : A blanket and a pillow, please.

B : Here they are.

A : Are these free? I want to lie down here.

B : Sure. You can take the arm off, if you want, then you can have a nice sleep, I think.

Dialog 2

A : What is the local time in New York now?

B : Well, it's two in the morning.

A : And what's our estimated time of arrival in New York?

B : 6 a.m.

A : What's the weather like there today?

B : We'll have a good weather in New York, sir.

local time : 현지시각.
E.T.A.(=estimated time of arrival) : 도착 예정시각.
E.T.D.(=estimated time of departure) : 출발 예정시각.

Dialog 3

A : What's this?

B : We have an American movie today.

A : That's good. What's the name of the movie?

B : "The Fight" starring Charles Bronson.

A : Oh, I like him. I'll bring you an earphone later.

B : You can enjoy stereo music too, if you want.

A : Thank you.

B : This is your earphone, sir. And here's your outlet.

A : What channel is the movie on?

B : Channel one.

Useful Expressions

1. What's the actual flying time from here to London?

2. What channel is the movie on?

3. What time does the program start?

4. It starts at 7:30.

5. It will start in 30 minutes.

6. Are we losing or gaining a day on the way to the States?

7. What's the time difference between Seoul and Singapore?

actual flying time : '실제 비행 시간'으로 항공기가 공중에 떠서 비행하는 총 시간을 말한다. 'local time'(현지시각)이 다를 수 있고, 또 중간 지점 등에서 체류한 시간이 있을 때 실제 비행한 시간만을 알려고 할 때 쓰는 용어.
time difference : 시차

Unit 9 LANDING

■A = Mr. Brown, ■B = Mr. Lee

Dialog 1

A : We're in Korea at last. This is where we have to say good-bye, Mr. Lee.

B : I hope you enjoyed your flight.

A : Yes, indeed, thanks for a first-rate plane service, and for your very pleasant company.

B : We must meet again.

A : Yes, we must. Well, good-bye.

Dialog 2

A : It was a smooth landing, wasn't it?

B : Yes, sure it was. Did you enjoy your flight?

A : Yes. You are the first Korean I saw on flight in my trip and I hope I can see you again.

B : Yes, we are in Korea at last. Well, I have to say good-bye now, Thomas.

A : Yes, we must. I'm glad to meet you.

B : Good-bye.

Useful Expressions

1. I enjoyed this flight.
2. I must get off and change planes at Kimpo.
3. Which is the first available connecting flight?
4. Have you ever been up in an airplane?
5. Yes, I've often flown to the United States.
6. It's a small world, isn't it?

It's a small word : 또 만났군요(다시 만났을 때 흔히 It's a small world, isn't it ?라는 고상한 표현을 쓴다)

Unit 10 CHECKING-OUT(At the Airport)

■A = Immigration Officer, ■B = Passenger

Dialog 1

A : May I see your passport, please?

B : Here you are.

A : And your vaccination certificate, please. How long are you going to stay in Korea, sir?

B : About two weeks.

A : Where will you be staying?

B : I'll be staying at Hilton Hotel.

A : What's the purpose of your visit?

B : For sightseeing.

A : O.K., that's all. Have a nice stay.

vaccination certificate : 전염병 예방접종증명서.
declare : 신고하다.
customs declaration form : 세관신고서.
personal effects : 개인용품.
purpose of the visit / trip : 여행(방문)목적.

■A = Customs Officer, ■B = Passenger

Dialog 2

A : Anything to declare?

B : No, nothing.

A : What's this?

B : This is my camera. I use it myself.

A : Any liquor, cigarettes, or gifts?

B : I have three bottles of whisky and some gifts for my friends here.

A : Do you have your customs declaration form?

B : Here it is.

Dialog 3

A : Do you have anything to declare?

B : No, I don't think so.

A : Will you open your bag?

B : Yes, certainly, sir. Here's my bag.

A : Are these all your personal effects?

B : Yes, these are all I have. But I have some cigarettes.

A : Okay. You may close your bag now.

B : Thank you, sir.

A : Have a nice trip!

Useful Expressions

1. How long are you going to stay in Korea?
2. Where will you be staying?
3. Are they strict at the customs house?
4. Do you have anything to declare?
5. They are tobacco, spirits, silks, jewels, watches, cameras, and so forth.
6. Are you disembarkation passengers?
7. How many pieces of luggage do you have?
8. Are there duty-free shops in the departure lounge?
9. What's the main purpose of your visit ?

disembarkation passenger : 입국 승객.
liquor : 독한 증류수(beer, wine에 대하여 brandy, whisky 따위).
liquer : 달고 향기 있는 독한 술.

Unit 11

MEETING SERVICE AT THE AIRPORT

▪A = Tour Guide, ▪B = Tourist

Dialog 1

A : Excuse me, but aren't you Mr. Brown from the States.

B : Yes, I am.

A : I am Mr. Kim from Korea Travel Service. I am here to meet you. Welcome to Seoul.

B : Well. How do you do, Mr. Kim. I didn't expect anyone to meet me at the airport. What a pleasant surprise. Thank you anyway for coming out here to meet me.

A : Nice to meet you. How was your trip?

B : A very good trip.

Dialog 2

A : At which hotel are you going to stay?

B : Hilton Hotel.

A : That's one of the best hotels in Seoul. I will give you a ride to your hotel.

B : Oh, will you?... Thanks a lot.

A : Are these all your baggage you have?

B : Yes, that's all.

Dialog 3

A : Excuse me. I believe you are Mr. Baker.

B : Yes, I am. Who are you?

A : I am Miss Oh from Korea Tourist Service. And I am here to meet you.

B : Oh, How do you do, Miss Oh? Nice to meet you. This is Mr. Smith.

A : Hello, Mr. Smith. Welcome to Seoul! Did you have a nice trip?

B : Yes, I did. It was a really good trip.

A : Then, shall we go out and take the bus. Come this way, please.

Useful Expressions

1. You are Mr. Baker, aren't you?
2. I'm here to meet you.
3. Nice to meet you.
4. Did you have a nice trip? 5. Did you enjoy your flight?
6. How did you find your trip to Kyongju?
7. Do you mind if I adjust the time of tomorrow's city tour with the guide?
8. I'll get in touch with the local operations if any changes come up.

Unit 12

USEFUL EXPRESSIONS

1. This is Mr. Park speaking.
2. Would you please hang up and call again?
3. Would you speak more slowly, please?
4. I'll get you Mr. Kim who speaks English.
5. He is not in at the moment.
6. May I have him return your call?/Shall I......
7. Is this Mr. Brown's residence?
8. You have the wrong number. Just a moment, I'll give you the correct number.
9. May I have your phone number, please?
10. May I speak to Mr. Johnson?
11. May I ask who is calling, please?
12. Thank you for calling Japan Air Lines.
13. Good morning. Domestic Reservations. May I help you?
14. You are Mr. Chang from Korea, aren't you?
15. Would you prefer a morning to an afternoon flight?
16. One moment, please. I'll check for you.

17. Thank you for waiting. I can make a reservation for you on Flight 311 which leaves at three o'clock.

18. Will that be all right?

19. May I have your name and phone number, please?

20. How do you spell your last name?

21. Your reservation number is 303.

22. You will need this number when you purchase your ticket.

23. You may purchase your ticket at any of our ticket offices.

24. Thank you for calling, sir.

25. We have three flights to Sydney at 10:00a.m., 12 noon, and two p.m.

26. Would you like to make a reservation? Did you make a reservation?

27. Is that a home phone or a business phone?

28. Would you like a round trip ticket or a one-way ticket?

29. May I issue a ticket for you now, sir?

30. Would you please fill out this form with your name and telephone number?

31. A one-way ticket to Cheju costs ₩74,900, sir.

32. Have you made a reservation yet, sir?

33. The ticket will be ₩74,900, sir.

34. Thank you, sir. That will be ₩5,100 in change.

35. Here's your ticket, sir, and here's your change.

36. Please check it, sir.

37. Please come to the airport at least twenty minutes before flight time.

38. Thank you, sir. Have a good flight.

39. We offer a 90% discount for infants.

40. We can accept American Express Cards for the ticket.

41. How long would you like to extend your ticket?

42. Please have your ticket endorsed to Korean Air Lines.

43. Don't forget to bring your refund sheets.

44. When and where did you lose the ticket?

45. May I see your ticket and passport, please?

46. Would you like a seat in the smoking or nonsmoking section, sir?

47. Please go upstairs and through gate 1 or 2 to the departure inspection area.

48. Do you have any baggage to check?

49. Is that all the baggage you have?

50. Thank you. Your documents are all in order, sir.

51. This is your boarding pass and here are your baggage claim tags.

52. Please present these tags to reclaim your baggage in Chicago.

53. Your seat number is 27A.

54. The flight will leave on time at ten o'clock from gate 23.

55. We will start the customs clearance about one hour before departure, and the boarding time will be about thirty minutes before departure.

56. Be sure to reconfirm your reservations 72 hours before departure.

57. I'm sorry, sir, but the flight is fully booked.

58. Would you like me to put you on the waiting list, sir?

59. What's the local time in Chicago?

60. Would you please trade seats with me? If we can be of service to you in any way, please push the button just above your head.

- **I'll get you Mr. Kim who speak English.** : 영어를 잘하는 Mr. Kim을 바꿔드리죠.
- **issue a ticket** : 발권하다.
- air ticket과 boarding pass(탑승권)를 혼동하지 않도록; air ticket는 항공기 여행의 전 일정에 대해 지불한 영수증(receipt)이고, 좌석번호(seat number)가 확정되어 탑승기에 오를 때 사용하는 것이 boarding pass이다.

PART II
HOTEL SERVICE

Unit 1 RESERVATION CLERK

■A = Guest, ■B = Clerk

Dialog 1

A : Hello, is this Hana Hotel?

B : Yes, can I help you, sir?

A : Yes, please. Can I put up at your hotel tonight?

B : Certainly, sir. What kind of room would you like to have?

A : A double room with bath, please.

B : Very good, sir.

A : I'll take it.

B : Thank you, sir. May I have your name, please?

A : Mr. and Mrs. Brown. We are from Chicago.

B : I see. How long are you going to stay here?

A : About a week.

B : Thanks for calling.

This is Mr. James speaking : 저는 미스터 제임스입니다.
I'd like to ~ : 「~하고 싶다」 want to 보다 정중한 표현.
put up at : 묵다, 투숙하다(lodge).

• 객실 종류
single room : 1인용 객실로 bed가 1개 있다.
twin room : 2인용 객실로 single bed가 2개 있다.
double room : 2인용 객실로 2인용의 커다란 double bed가 1개 있다.
triple room : 3인용 객실로 single bed가 3개 있다.
suite : 특실로서 sitting room(응접실), bedroom(침실), 큰 bathroom, kitchen 등의 시설이 있어 하나의 apartment의 맛을 풍기고 있다.

Dialog 2

A : Hello, this is Mr. James speaking. Is this Hilton Hotel?
B : Yes, sir.
A : I'd like to get a room.
B : Thank you very much. What kind of room would you like, sir?
A : A single room with bath, please.
B : Very good, sir. We have a nice room available.
A : I'll take it. I'll be there shortly.
B : Yes, sir. We will be waiting for you.

▪A = Clerk, ▪B = Guest

Dialog 3

A : Reservation desk. Miss Kim speaking. May I help you?
B : This is C & G Corporation in Seoul. I'd like to make a reservation.
A : May I have your name and phone number, please?
B : Thomas Smith. 312-1234.

May 1st through May 3rd : 5월 1일부터 계속해서 5월 3일까지.
room rate : 객실료.
service charge : 봉사료.
May I have your name? : 성함이 무엇입니까?(What's your name은 피하는 것이 좋다).
make a reservation : 예약을 하다.

A : What kind of room would you like, sir?
B : A double room with bath, please.
A : How long are you going to stay here, sir?
B : I want to stay from May 1st through May 3rd.
A : Thank you for calling. We'll expect you.

Dialog 4

A : Good morning, this is reservation, Lotte Hotel. May I help you?
B : Yes, this is Mr. Smith, I have just arrived at the airport. Do you have a single for tonight and tomorrow night?
A : Yes, sir. We have a single room with bath.
B : What is the room rate?
A : 261 dollars per night. The government tax and service charges will be added to this rate.
B : What are added?
A : The tax and service charges.
B : How much is it?
A : About 21%.
B : Very good. I'll take it. My name is Mr. William H. Smith from Los Angeles. I'll be at the hotel by six o'clock.

객실료(room rate)를 계산할 때 주의할 일은 객실료에 봉사료(service charge) 10%를 더한 후 세금 10%(tax)를 더하기 때문에 객실료 + 약 21%가 실제 지불하는 금액임을 유의하도록.

Useful Expressions

1. I'd like to make a reservation.

2. Haven't you got any cheaper room?

3. Don't you have any vacant room?

4. We have lots of vacant rooms.

5. I'm sorry sir. We don't have any vacant rooms.
(= We don't have any room available.)

A Guide to Hospitality Industry

-Six Secrets of Successful Hotelmanship-

1. Always keep an eye on the balance sheet.
2. Don't promise more than you can deliver - deliver more than you promise.
3. Select the right personnel.
4. Use the "Personal Touch" to build loyalty among your guests.
5. Create a warm and welcoming hotel personality.
6. Cultivate the right attitude toward your position, your staff and your guests.

Unit 1 DOORPERSON

■A = Doorperson, ■B = Guest

Dialog 1

A : Good morning, sir. May I help you with your baggage?

B : No, it's all right. It's not heavy. So, I'll carry it by myself. Where can I register?

A : You can register at the front desk over there to your right.

B : Thank you.

A : Please watch out of the revolving door. The inside door is automatic.

B : Thank you.

Dialog 2

A : Good morning, sir. Are you leaving today?

B : Yes, I'm going to take the flight at one o'clock.

Where can I register? : 등록은 어디서 합니까?
watch out : 조심하다, 주의하다.
revolving door : 회전식문.
had better : ~하는 것이 좋다. 해야된다.
right away : 즉시.
'즉시'란 표현은 미인들은 흔히 'right away'나 'right now'를 영국계 사람들은 'at once'를 쓴다. 문어체에서는 흔히 'immediately'를 쓰고 있다.

A : Are you? It's ten past eleven now. I think you'd better hurry.

B : I have a black bag in front of the hotel room. Could you bring it to me?

A : Yes, sir. I'll load this baggage in the trunk.

Dialog 3

A : Good morning. May I help you, sir?

B : Yes. Can you call my car, please?

A : Yes, what's the number?

B : 3125.

A : Wait a minute, please. I'll call it right away.

Useful Expressions

1. Can you get me a taxi, please?

2. I'll call it right away.

3. Are you leaving today?

4. Good-bye. Please come again.

5. It's very hot, isn't it?

Unit 3 ROOM CLERK

■A = Room Clerk, ■B = Guest

Dialog 1

A : Good evening, sir. May I help you?
B : Good evening. I have a reservation here.
A : May I have your name, please?
B : Thomas Brown.
A : Oh, yes. We have your reservation. A single room with bath, room 1825.
B : That's fine.
A : Would you fill out this form, please?
B : Here you are.
A : I hope you enjoy your stay here.
B : Thanks a lot.

fill out this form : 양식에 기입하다.
Here you are : 여기 있습니다. 'Here they are' 또는 'Here it is'의 표현도 있다.
register : 등록하다.
double bed : 2인용 단일침대.
single bed : 1인용 침대.
twin bed : 한방에 single bed가 2개.
※ 대단히 고맙다고 할 때 'Thank you very much' 또는 'thanks a lot'를 쓰는데 후자의 표현은 극히 informal 하기 때문에 손윗사람이나 친숙하지 않은 사람에게겐 쓰지 않는 것이 좋다.

Dialog 2

A : Good evening. sir. May I help you?

B : Yes, please. Do you have a room.

A : Yes, we do. A double or a single.

B : A single.

A : How long will you be staying, sir.

B : Just for tonight. I'm going to Gyeongju tomorrow.

A : Very well, sir. Would you please register?

B : Here you are.

A : And the bellperson will show you to your room. Have a nice day.

B : Thanks a lot.

Dialog 3

A : May I have your name, sir?

B : My name is Thomas Brown.

A : Just a moment, please.... Yes, that's right. We have your reservation. How long are you staying, sir?

B : I'm staying for two nights. What's the rate of a single room with bath per day?

A : We have a good single room with bath for 53 dollars per day.

B : That'll be fine. And I want a quiet room.

A : Of course you can have a very quiet room. It's on the 16th floor with a nice view. Will you register here, please?

B : All right.

A : Here's your key. Your room number is 1666. The porter will carry your baggage.

B : Thank you.

Dialog 4

A : Good morning, sir. Welcome to Hilton Hotel. May I help you?

B : I want a room for the next ten days. Do you have one?

A : Do you have a reservation, sir?

B : No, I don't.

A : Just a moment, sir. I'll check to see if we have a room available. Would a studio twin room be all right, sir?

B : What's studio twin room?

A : It's a twin room with a studio bed that can fold up into a sofa.

B : That will be fine.

A : We do not have any room available for a full ten nights. (We don't have any rooms available for such a period.) Would you mind changing rooms in the middle of your stay?

B : No, it's all right with me.

A : Thank you, sir. Would you please register here? Please be sure to fill in everything.

B : All right. Here you are.

A : Thank you, sir. A bellperson will show you to your room.

Useful Expressions

1. Please register here, sir.

2. I have a reservation at this hotel.

3. We have your reservation.

4. How long are you staying, sir?

5. I'm staying two nights.

6. What's the rate of a single room?

- **register** : 숙박부에 인적사항을 기록하다.
- 우편물에서 'registered mail'하면 등기우편을 말한다.

Unit 4 BELLPERSON

■A = Bellperson, ■B = Guest, C = Clerk

Dialog 1

A : Your baggage, please?

B : This bag, suit case, and that golf club bag there.

A : Any other baggage coming, sir?

B : Yes, I've got two more pieces coming.

A : Now, this way, please.

B : This room looks all right.

A : Thank you, sir. Built-in closet here and bathroom over there.

B : I want to send a cable. Will you get me a cable form?

A : All stationery is in this desk drawer, sir.

B : That's fine.

A : Anything else (I can do), sir?

B : No, I guess that's all.

built-in closet : 붙박이 벽장.
built-in-table : 붙박이 식탁.
bathroom : 욕실, 화장실.
cable : 전보.
stationery : 문구류.
desk drawer : 책상서랍.

Dialog 2

A : There is a beauty parlor and barber's in the first basement, sir.

B : How late do they stay open?

A : Until 8 o'clock, sir.

B : Thanks. That gives us plenty of time.

A : Here is your room. sir. Closet with clothes hangers here, and here is the bathroom. Stationery, room service menu and a brochure giving all the services of the hotel are in this desk. Light switches here and thermostat.

B : Thank you.

Dialog 3

A : This is where we get off. Down this way, please.

B : This is a nice room, isn't it? I think we ought to be comfortable here.

B : This is for you.

A : I'm sorry, but, no tipping is our pride. If you need anything, just call the desk.

clothes hanger : 옷걸이.
brochure : =pamphlet ; 안내책자.
thermostat : 지동 온도 조절 장치. thermos(보온병)와 구별할 것.

Dialog 4

C : (Calls for a bellperson) Show Mr. Brown to room 714.

A : Yes, sir. Are these your bags?

B : Yes, they are.

A : This way please. Here we are 714. (Bellperson opens the door.)

A : Here's the light switch for the bathroom, the radio and the air conditioning. The TV set, as you can see here, and the switch is on the right side of the set.

B : Is it a sunny room?

A : No, sir. The sun never visits, but it commands a fine view of the river.

Useful Expressions

1. Any other baggage coming?
2. Yes, I have two more coming.
3. Will you get me a messenger service?
4. Is your faucet water fit to drink?
5. That's all for the time being.

The sun never visits : 햇살이 전혀 들지 않는다.
commands a fine view : 경관이 좋다.
for the time being : 당분간
fit to drink : 음료수로 적합하다.

Unit 5 TELEPHONE OPERATOR

■A = Telephone operator, ■B = Guest

Dialog 1

A : Good evening. This is operator speaking, sir.

B : Is this the operator? This is Wilson in room 1825 speaking.

A : What can I do for you, Mr. Wilson?

B : Can you give me a morning call at 6:30?

A : Yes, sir. Mr. Wilson in room 1825, morning call at 6:30.

B : Wilson speaking.

A : Good morning, Mr. Wilson. It is 6:30 now.

Dialog 2

A : Good morning. Operator.

B : Hello? Could you get me 452-7955, please.

A : Yes. sir. One moment, please.

B : Shall I hold the line or hang up?

morning call : 아침 시각을 알려주는 전화 즉 기상전화, wake up call이라고도 한다.
get me ～ : ～대주다(전화).
Shall I hold the line or hang up? : 수화기를 들고 기다릴까요 끊을까요?(전화).
overseas call : 국제전화.

A : Please hold the line... I'm sorry, sir, but your party doesn't answer.

B : Well, never mind. I'll try again later.

■A = Guest, ■B = Operator

Dialog 3

A : Operator? I'd like to make an overseas call to New York.

B : Is it a person-to-person call, sir?

A : Yes. The party I want to call is Mr. Philip Dawson. The number is 542-7962.

B : Mr. Philip Dawson, New York 542-7962 ?

A : Yes, that's right.

B : It may take about fifteen minutes. Will you be in your room, sir?

A : I'd like to take the call in the main dining room.

B : Very well, sir. Please tell the head waiter that you are expecting a call.

I'm sorry is used when apologizing.

Ex. I'm sorry to have kept you waiting so long.

I'm sorry to say is used to inform someone of bad news.

Ex. I'm sorry to say that your daughter will have to spend about a month in the hospital.

Your party doesn't answer : 상대방이 전화 받지 않는데요.

person-to-person call : 지명인 전화(지정인이 없을 때는 전화료를 묻지 않는다).

station-to station call : 대국 전화(전화번호에서 아무라도 응답이 있으면 통화로 간주).

■A = Operator, ■B = Guest

Dialog 4

A : Operator. Prince Hotel, May I help you?
B : I want to speak to Mr. Custer, room 468, please.
A : Room 468? One moment please. (The operator connects this call to 468)
A : Operator, Prince Hotel, can I help you?
B : How can I call this phone number Seoul 221-4061?
A : Please dial zero first and then the number you want.
B : I see, thanks.
A : Prince Hotel operator, may I help you?
B : This is Wood, room 725. Would you wake me up at six thirty tomorrow morning, please?
A : Mr. Wood, room 725, six thirty, call tomorrow morning?
B : Yes, please.
A : Very well, sir. Good night.

Useful Expressions

1. The line is out of order. (= The line broke down.)
2. The line is dead.
3. The line is crossed.
4. We had a bad connection.
5. I'm sorry, I must have dialed the wrong number.

6. I'd like to make a long distance call to Pusan.

7. I'd like to make an overseas call to New York.

8. Mr. Lee is talking on another phone. (= He's on the other phone.)

9. Shall I have him call you when he comes in? (= Would you like him to call you when he gets back?)

10. I am sorry, but he is in conference right now.

11. He is away just now. (= He is not in at the moment. He is out at the moment.)

12. Who would you like to speak to?

13. How soon will he be back? What time is he expected back? Can I expect him shortly?

14. She will be with you in a minute.

15. Will you get me extension 6711. I'll get you his division.

16. Who am I speaking with (to)? (= Who am I) talking to?) (= Who is this speaking? Who is this calling? Who's calling, please?)

17. This number doesn't ring a bell. (= This number doesn't sound familiar to me.)

18. Where do you think I can reach him right now? Would you like to leave a message? (= May I take your message?)

19. There is no one here by that name. (= There isn't anyone here by that name.)

20. You are wanted on the phone. (= A phone call for you.) (= You have a call.)

21. Could you speak up, please. (= Please speak a little louder.)

22. What is this regarding? (= What is this concerning? What is this call about?)

23. Can I have an emergency call to this number? Do you wish to release the line?

24. Are you the same person I just talked to? (= Are you the same person I talked to a moment ago?)

25. The line is continuously busy and I can't get through.

26. I'm returning Mr. Beston's call. May I speak with him?

27. I don't recognize your voice. I recognized him immediately.

28. I have to get off the telephone now. (= I have to hang up now. I have to end our conversation now.)

29. Would you like to speak to someone else?

30. Will you accept a collect call from Miss Rosemarie Beston in Columbia, Missouri?

31. No one answered the phone. (= There was no answer.)

What is this regarding?(용건이 무엇입니까?)에 대한 응답의 한 예는 다음과 같다. /This is regarding our appointment. (약속 때문에 전화드립니다.)
This number dosen't ring a bell : 이 전화번호는 누구 것인지 모르겠는데.
accept a collect call : 수신인 요금부담의 전화를 받겠다.

Unit 6 INFORMATION CLERK

▪A = Guest, ▪B = Clerk

Dialog 1

A : May I have some information on the night club?

B : Yes, sir.

A : Can you describe it in general?

B : Yes, it is located in the basement and open from 7 p.m. till 2 in the morning. You can enjoy delightful music.

A : What time did you say the night club is closed?

B : It's closed at two o'clock in the morning, sir.

A : That's good. Can you make a reservation right now?

B : Yes, sir.

Dialog 2

A : I heard that the Korean Folk Village is famous. How can I get there?

B : We have a shuttle bus going there, but it would be difficult for a foreigner to take it.

B : I would like to suggest that you either rent a car or use a tour bus of a travel agency.

Folk Village : 민속촌.
shuttle bus : 정기 노선 버스.

A : It sounds very interesting. Can you reserve a taxi immediately?

B : Certainly, sir. What time will you leave, sir?

A : It's 8:40 now. I would like to leave at nine.

B : Fine. Please come back at nine.

A : I see. It is very kind of you.

Dialog 3

A : Can you recommend some place for our dinner?

B : Why don't you have your dinner at the Korean Restaurant on the 7th floor.

A : Should I make a reservation?

B : Yes, sir. You had better make a reservation.

A : Will you put me on the reservation list?

B : Yes, sir. May I have your name, please?

A : My name is Thomas Brown.

Dialog 4

A : When is check out time?

B : Check out time is 12:00 noon, sir.

check out time : 퇴숙시간(일반적으로 낮 12시 : twelve noon).
extra room charge : 별도(추가)객실요금.

A : What are the extra room charge?

B : If you check in before 05:00 a.m., there is one day's charge. If you check in from 05:00 a.m. until 11:00 a.m., there's a 30% of one day's charge.

A : Do you offer any room service?

B : Yes, sir. Room service is available from 07:00 a.m. until 10:00 p.m. Just dial 5 for room service.

A : I's there a service charge for room service?

B : Yes, sir. A 10% service charge.

A : What's your laundry service hours?

B : If your laundry is received before 10:00 a.m., We deliver it by 10:00 p.m. the same day. If you bring it before 3:00 p.m., we will get it back by noon the next day.

A : Who shall I call?

B : Please call the room maid.

A : Does she handle the dry cleaning and pressing?

B : Yes, sir.

A : Who do I call for morning call, please?

B : Please call the switch board (dial 9, please).

Why don't you …? : '~를 하시지요.'라고 권유할 때 쓰는 부드러운 표현.
Why don't you go to the party at the church?

Useful Expressions

1. Why don't you take the city tour bus?
2. Can you explain it in detail?
3. It sounds interesting!
4. How can I get to the American Embassy?
5. It takes 10 minutes by taxi.
6. Until what time are the shops in the arcade open?
7. I'd like to see the person in charge of banquet service about a conference room.

• person in charge는 책임자란 의미로, "Who is the person in charge?"라고 하면 책임자를 묻는 것이고, "Who is the manager?"라고 하면 지배인을 찾는 경우가 되겠다.
• Room charge : 연회 등 회의장을 빌리 때 식사를 하게되면 room charge는 무료로 해주곤 한다. 이때 공짜란 말은 영어로 "free of charge", 또는 "gratis"란 말이 있으나 무료를 "service"로 해준다고 하면 영어로선 오류를 범하게 된다.
• "Compliment of / this hotel"
/ KAL이라고 하면 이 호텔에서 또는 KAL회사에서 베푸는 무료 은전을 말한다. "a complimentary ticket"라고 하면(음악회 등의) 우대권 · 초대권을 말한다.

Unit 7

MAIL CLERK

■A = Guest, ■B = Clerk

Dialog 1

A : What is the postal charge for this letter? It is for the U.S.A.

B : It seems to be heavy. Let me weigh it first. It is 17 grams. The basic charge for the American area is 450 won. It costs 540 won from 10 grams up to 20 grams, sir.

A : Please give me 540 won worth of stamps.

B : If you will give the postal charge and letter to me, I'll be glad to mail it for you. I stop by the post office twice a day.

Dialog 2

A : Is there any mail for me? Room 905.

B : How are you, Mr. Smith. We do not have any mail for you, sir.

A : I am supposed to have important document. What is your mail delivery time?

B : Ten o'clock a.m. and three p.m. twice a day. sir.

postal charge : 우편요금, 체송료

Dialog 3

A : Any mail for me?

B : We have just received letters. Let me check it.

A : I'm waiting for letters, you know.

B : Here they are.

A : Thanks a lot.

Dialog 4

A : Would you give this message to Mrs. Kim?

B : Certainly. What's her room number, please? ,

A : I don't remember, but I think she is on the fifth floor.

B : That's all right. I'll look it up. How do you spell her name?

A : K.I.M. Kim.

B : Oh, yes, here it is. Room 508. I'll see that she gets the message.

Useful Expressions

1. Will you post this letter? Will you please mail this letter for me?

2. I'll mail your letter.

3. Let me weigh it.

4. I'll be glad to mail it for you.

5. Will you please do that for me?

6. Until what time is the post office in the hotel open?

•카운터에서

현관에서 카운터(또는 프런트데스크)까지는 보이(급사)가 짐을 날라다 준다. 잊지 말고 팁을 주도록 하라. front desk에서 담당직원에서 자기 이름을 대고 예약을 확인하다. 이때, 요금이나 욕실의 유무 등을 확인하며, 사양말고 자신의 요구를 말하도록 하라. 묵을 방이 정해지면 등록(Registration)을 한다. 즉 카드에 이름과 주소를 쓴다. 그것이 끝나면 담당직원이 벨을 눌러 bell person(담당 급사)를 부른다.

•방으로

Bellperson이 짐을 가지고 방으로 안내한다. suitcase 등은 짐 두는데 놓고, 코트가 있으면 옷걸이에 걸고 실내온도를 조절해 준다. 일을 마치고 bellperson이 나갈 때 팁을 준다.

•호텔의 열쇠

방을 나올 때나 잠잘 때에는 반드시 도어를 잠그도록 해야하는 것은 두말할 나위 없지만, 자동적으로 도어가 잠기도록 되어 있는 문이 많으므로 방안에 열쇠를 두고 나가는 일이 없도록 조심해야 한다.

•호텔의 복도

간혹 잠옷바람이나 실내화를 신고 호텔의 복도로 나가는 사람이 있는데, 이것은 큰 실례이니 삼가도록 한다. 호텔의 복도는 바깥 한길과 같다고 생각하면 그런 실수는 범하지 않게 된다.

•호텔의 식사

호텔 안의 식당도 바깥의 식당과 마찬가지로 생각하여 옷차림을 단정히 한다. 조반은 호텔에서 드는 일이 많은데 유럽에서는 가벼운 아침 식사가 보통이며, 빵과 잼 · 버터, 그리고 홍차나 커피 · 우유 등의 음료가 곁들여지는 정도이다. 미국에서는 위에 든 것 이외에, 주스 · 곡류 식품(콘플레이크 따위) · 달걀 요리가 더 나온다. 달걀요리는 어떻게 해 달라고 요구한다.

•check out(퇴숙 수속)

카운터에 전화로 연락해서 부탁하면 포터(porter)가 짐을 가지러 온다(팁이 필요). 택시도 카운터에 부탁하면 수배해 준다. 숙박료 지불은 「CASHIER(금전출납원)」라는 표시가 있는 데로 가서 방 열쇠를 돌려주고 청산한다.

•check out time

방을 내주어야 할 시간인데, 대개 정오 때쯤이다. 이 시간이 넘으면 추가 요금을 물게되므로 미리 호텔의 check out 시각을 확인해 둘 필요가 있다.

Unit 8 CHECKROOM ATTENDANT

■A = Checkroom attendant, ■B = Guest

Dialog 1

A : How are you, sir? Are you leaving today?

B : Yes, I am leaving today. I'd like to have this baggage kept here for a while.

A : Certainly, sir. When will you want it back, sir?

B : The plane will depart at 7 o'clock. As you know, the check-out time is 12 noon.

A : You are right, sir. If you should stay in your room till then, you would have to pay extra charge, sir.

B : I still have something to do. I'll be back by 4 o'clock.

A : I see. Here is your baggage ticket, sir.

Dialog 2

A : May I help you, sir?

B : Yes. I lost my baggage ticket.

check room : =cloakroom ; 휴대품 보관실.
checkroom attendant : 휴대품 보관소 직원.
I'd like to have this baggage kept here for a while : 잠시 이 짐을 보관하고자 합니다.
다음과 같은 표현도 있다. Can I check my baggage until this evening?

A : That is a problem. Can you remember the checking date?

B : It was on March 5th, the day I went down to Pusan.

A : I hope your baggage is safe. Let's see the list. May I have your name, please?

B : My name is Reed. I stayed in room 905.

A : Here it is. Fortunately, your baggage was not yet claimed.

Dialog 3

B : One black travel bag and one case containing sample. The case is this big, you know.

A : You seem to be the owner according to what you have said. Could you identify yourself?

B : Yes, I will. Here is my passport. You can believe that I am Reed.

A : Thank you. Wait a minute, sir. First, I have to report it to my supervisor and follow his direction, sir. Sorry to have kept you waiting, sir. We have no doubt the baggage belongs to you. It was just a procedure for safe handling, sir. I hope you don't mind.

Useful Expressions

1. Please keep this baggage.
2. Are you leaving today?
3. The check-out time is 12 noon.
4. I'll be back by 3 o'clock.
5. I'll keep it for you.
6. Why don't you check at the lost & found office?

lost & found office : 분실물 취급소.

Unit 9 FRONT CASHIER

▪A = Cashier, ▪B = Guest

Dialog 1

A : May I help you?

B : Yes, I'd like to pay my account, room 1525.

A : Certainly, sir. I won't keep you one moment... This is the total, sir, four hundred thousand won.

B : I'd like to have this charged to my account. I've been a guest at your hotel on many occasions, and I've established credit arrangements with you.

A : Yes, sir. Will you sign the account, while I take down name and address? Thank you, sir.

B : Thanks. Good-bye.

A : Good-bye, sir.

- **Front Service** : 서구 호텔 front service로는 front desk(reception desk라고도 함)가 있어 방의 업무, key 관리, message 전달 등의 업무를 보며, cashier는 주로 회계 출납 업무를 본다. bell captain's desk에서는 수하물의 운반으로부터 시내 안내(city information)에 이르기까지 여러 가지의 service 제공을 해주며, assistant manager는 lobby에 desk를 놓고 사소한 상담까지 service를 해 준다.

checking-out : 계산을 마치고 퇴숙하는 것.
receipt : 영수증.
bill : 청구서, 계산서.

■A = Guest, ■B = Cashier

Dialog 2

A : I am Baker in room 905. I am checking out today. Will you make out my bill?

B : Wait a moment, sir. It comes to a total of 238,800 won, sir.

A : Here you are.

B : Here is your change, 1,200 won, sir.

A : That is for you, though it is a small amount. I don't need it, anyway.

B : Thank you. Here is your receipt, sir.

A : Thank you. I have enjoyed my stay here. Good bye.

B : Good bye, sir. Please come again.

Dialog 3

A : Yes, we are checking out. We have to catch a plane at 12:30. How much is our bill?

B : Just a moment, sir. Here it is, sir. Fifty three thousand two hundred twenty five won.

A : I don't have that much won on me. I'll have to give you part of it in dollars. Let's see, here is one hundred dollars and ten thousand won. Will that do?

B : Yes, sir. Here is your change. I hope you enjoyed your stay. Please come again.

Useful Expressions

1. I'd like to pay my account, room 510.
2. I won't keep you one moment.
3. I'd like to have this charged to my account.
4. I have (established) credit arrangements with you.
5. Can I exchange some dollars?
6. Can I exchange some traveler's checks?
7. I'm afraid you'll have to vacate your room by twelve noon, sir. Otherwise, we'll have to charge you for another day.
8. We'll deduct that amount from the total charge when you pay tomorrow morning.

- 계산을 치르는 방법은 두가지가 있어 cashier가 묻게 된다. Everybody will come here to pay for his/her bill. 각자 다 와서 자기분을 지불할 겁니다.
  ① Does everybody pay for his incidental charges?(개인 계산은 각자가 지불 할 건가요?)
  ② Do you want the charge billed to your master account?(선생님 앞으로 단체 계산을 하도록 하시겠습니까?)
  위 ①과 같이 단체 여행시도 개인적으로 사용한 계산을 각자가 하는 경우가 있고, ②와 같이 일단 단체로 계산하고 후에 차내에서나 여가가 있을 때 걷어들이는 방법이 있는데, 국외 여행시는 ②의 방법이 번거로움을 덜어주는 고로 흔히 그렇게들 한다.
- 다음 각 객실에서 챙긴 짐을 처리하는 방법인데, Shall we put our baggage outside the room?(우리 짐을 밖에 내어놓을까요?) 위 문장처럼 짐을 객실 밖 lobby 등으로 내어놓을지 아니면 room 안에 놓을지를 미리 타진해서 일행에게 일러두는 것도 인솔자로서 할 일이다.

vacate one's room : 방을 비워 주다.(check-out time 까지 객실을 비우지 않으면 하루 객실료를 더 부담하는 수가 있으니 미리 check-out time을 알라 둘 필요가 있다).

Unit 10 HOUSEKEEPER

■A = Clerk, ■B = Guest

Dialog 1

A : This is the housekeeping clerk speaking. Can I help you, sir?

B : This is Martin, room 707. The room is not warm enough. I am worried I might catch a cold.

A : There is a heating controller on the wall. Is it properly adjusted?

B : I know how to handle the controller. It is still cold though I adjusted it to highest.

A : Our engineer will be there within five minutes, sir.

Dialog 2

B : This is room 1007. I have only five hangers. Can you send some more hangers.

A : Certainly. Are you in room 1007? Would three more hangers do?

B : Please send two more hangers and two more blankets.

A : I understand, sir. We will send additionally 2 hangers and 2 blankets to room 1007 right away.

heating controller : 온도 조절기.

Dialog 3

B : This is Mrs. Baker who stayed in room 1807 of your hotel. I am making a phone call from the airport now.

A : How are you Mrs. Baker? Aren't you calling because of the lost ring in room 1803?

B : Yes. Have you found it?

A : Yes, the room maid brought it. You left it on the dresser. We are keeping it at the lost and found section, ma'am.

Dialog 4

A : This is housekeeping. May I help you?

B : Yes, I'll be out for half an hour. I expect Mr. Thomas to come while I'm out. Let him in and have him wait.

A : I'm sorry, sir. We cannot let someone else into your room. Would you like me to have him wait in the lobby on the first floor?

B : Yes. I suppose so. Also, would you fix the desk lamp in my room? It seems to be little dim.

A : Yes, sir. I'll have it taken care of right away. Is there anything else?

B : No, that's all. But try to have it done before I'm back.

A : Yes, sir.

Useful Expressions

1. I'm going to take a bath.
2. I'll take care of it right away.
3. Housekeeping clerk speaking. May I help you, sir?
4. We'll send you two more blankets.
5. We'll bring it to you at once.

Unit 11 ROOMMAID

▪A = Guest, ▪B = Roommaid

Dialog 1

A : Sorry to have called you. Can you bring some water in the water pitcher?

B : Oh, my goodness! I forgot to fill the water pitcher.

A : No, it was full, but I drank it all as I was very thirsty.

B : I see. I will bring it to you in a moment.

A : Would you go out of your way to bring me some ice water instead of hot water?

B : Yes, sir.

Dialog 2

B : Are you leaving today?

A : Yes, I appreciate your special care during my stay here.

B : You have lots of things to pack up. May I help you?

A : Thank you. I have to count on your help even at my leaving time.

B : Was there anything uncomfortable during your stay?

A : I really enjoyed my stay. If I have another chance to visit Korea, I will be pleased to make arrangements for my stay in your hotel.

Dialog 3

A : Who is it?

B : Roommaid. Good morning, sir.

A : Good morning. Do you want anything?

B : If you don't mind, I would like to clean the room now.

A : Can you fix the room right now?

B : It will take about 15 minutes, sir.

A : You do a nice job, don't you?

▪A = Room Maid, ▪B = Guest

Dialog 4

A : Good morning, this is the maid.

B : Good morning, will you come to room 605 please? I have some laundry and dry cleaning.

A : Yes, sir.

B : These things are for the laundry, and these are for dry cleaning. Our valet has one or two hour quick service and a regular service. Would you like to have them back in a hurry?

B : No, not particularly. I will take the regular service. Two suits for dry cleaning, five pairs of shorts and undershirts, and three white shirts.

A : All right, sir. Please sign here.

B : Okay.

A : Thank you, sir.

Useful Expressions

1. How about going to the coffee shop in the mean time, sir?
2. See you later, sir.
3. Shall I pay for it now?
4. I'll clean the room.
5. Please do a good job.

in the mean time : (=for the mean time ; meanwhile) 그러는 사이, 그럭저럭 하는 동안에 ; 객실 청소를 하는 동안 coffee shop에 가서 차를 한잔 든다든지 할 때 쓰는 표현.

Unit 12 LAUNDRY CLERK

■A = Guest, ■B = Clerk

Dialog 1

A : I have to go to a party in this suit tonight. Can you make it by then?

B : I think this should be dry-cleaned. When do you want it to be delivered?

A : By six o'clock this evening.

B : You can get it by then, sir.

A : By the way, ask them to take this stain off, please.

B : Is this grease?

A : It might be fruit stain or something. I don't know exactly.

B : Whatever it is, I'll ask them to remove it completely.

Dialog 2

B : Laundry service, I have brought your laundry, sir.

A : Come in.

B : Yes, I believe you will be satisfied with them. Would you check the laundry, please?

B : Here is the laundry slip you signed yesterday.

A : I believe it's correct. Yes, it's correct.

laundry : 세탁소(물).
laundry slip : 세탁료.

B : Thank you. Here is your laundry bill. sir.

A : Should I pay in cash?

B : As you like, sir. You can pay in cash or sign for it so that you can pay later when you check out, sir.

A : Then, I'd like to sign for it.

B : Thank you. Have a good night's sleep, sir.

Dialog 3

A : When can I get it back, if I send out laundry today?

B : Are you in a hurry?

A : No, not especially, but...

B : Usually you can get it back on the following day. But, if rushed, you can get it in the evening. There is an extra charge, though.

A : There is no rush. Let me have the laundry slip.

B : Here it is.

A : Good. You wait here as it won't take me long to fill out.

B : Certainly.

Useful Expressions

1. Laundry service, sir. Have you got laundry?

2. Fill in the laundry slip, please.

3. When will I get it back? /When can I have the laundry returned?

4. Would you sign this, please?

Unit 13

RECEPTIONIST

▪A = Receptionist, ▪B = Guest

Dialog 1

A : Good evening, sir. Did you make a reservation, sir?

B : I am Baker, and this is my wife. We reserved a table this morning.

A : This way, please.

B : It's a marvelous restaurant. I think you have a lot of guests.

A : Thank you for your compliment, sir. Here is your table, sir.

Dialog 2

A : Good evening. May I help you, sir?

B : Do you have a table for two?

A : You don't have a reservation, do you?

B : No.

A : We don't have any vacant tables. Do you mind if you have to share a table, sir?

B : No, we don't.

Dialog 3

A : Good evening, sir? May I help you?

B : We have a reservation here. My name is Lyn Martin. A table for seven, please.

A : Would you follow me? Would you take those seats?

B : Fine. This table is O.K.

A : I hope you enjoy your dinner.

Useful Expressions

1. Do you have a reservation?
2. Would you wait a moment, please?
3. Your waitress will be with you in a minute.
4. Enjoy your food.
5. Would you follow me?

Unit 14 BREAKFAST(Waiter/Waitress)

■A = Guest, ■B = Waiter

Dialog 1

A : I'd like two eggs and coffee.

B : Boiled or fried?

A : Fried.

B : Sunny-side up or turned over?

A : Turned over, please. I want them hot, please.

■A = Waiter, ■B = Guest

Dialog 2

A : May I take your order, ma'am?

B : Yes. I'll have tomato juice, shredded wheat, and bacon and eggs.

A : Which would you prefer, tea or coffee?

B : Tea with milk, please.

A : How do you want your eggs?

B : Turned over, please.

sunny-side up : 한면만 반숙 후라이한 달걀.
turned over : 양면을 후라이한 달걀.
in cash : 현찰로.
traveler's check : 여행자수표(T/C)

A : Very well, ma'am.

B : Please rush my order. I have to be at the airport by eight thirty. Certainly, ma'am. I would appreciate it if you would pay for your breakfast in cash. That way, I won't have to bill you again.

Dialog 3

A : Good morning, sir. Here is the menu, sir. Would you like to have coffee first?

B : Now let me see... I'll have coffee, toast, a small glass of fresh orange juice, and ham and eggs.

A : Very well. Would you like to have some cereal ma'am?

B : Oh, yes, I would. Bring me corn flakes with raisins.

A : Yes, ma'am. How would you like your toast, dark or light?

B : I want my toast dark. Also, please bring me some marmalade.

A : Sure.

Dialog 4

A : Good morning, sir. Some fruit?

B : What have you got this morning?

A : Assorted fresh fruit and some stewed prunes and figs.

B : Stewed figs? Give me that and a glass of tomato juice.

A : Any cereal, sir?

B : Yes, a dish of cream of wheat. I like to have my coffee now, too.

A : Egg or something?
B : I'd like two eggs and coffee.
A : Boiled or fried?
B : Fried.
A : Sunny-side up or turned over?
B : Turned over, please. I want them hot please.

Useful Expressions

1. What would you like to have for breakfast?
2. Just coffee, please.
3. Anything else, sir?
4. What would you like to order?
5. May I take your order now?

Unit 15

LUNCHEON(Waiter/Waitress)

■A = Waiter, ■B = Guest

Dialog 1

A : Would you care for cocktail?

B : One Vodka Martini, one Bloody Mary and two Jin & Tonics, please.

A : Would you like to order now, sir?

B : Yes. one Lobster, one Scallop, one Filet Mignon, and one Sirloin Steak, please.

A : How would you like your steak, sir?

B : Medium rare, please.

A : Would you care for anything else?

B : Yes, I'd like some coffee, please.

A : Did you enjoy your food?

B : Yes, I enjoyed it very much.

A : Are you through, sir.

B : Yes, I'm done.

lobster : 바다가재.
scallop : 조갯살.
rare : 설익은, 덜구은(underdone)
medium : 중간쯤(보통)으로 구은.
raw : 날것.
Do you eat raw fish? : 생선회를 드십니까?

Dialog 2

A : What would you like to order, sir?

B : I want some spaghetti.

A : I'm sorry, spaghetti is not on the menu.

B : Can you make some for me?

A : Just a moment, please. I'll ask it. Yes, we can make some for you. It will take about 15 minutes. All right, sir?

B : That's all right.

A : What kind of sauce do you like?

B : Tomato sauce, please. Bring me a salad, too.

A : What kind of salad dressing, sir?

B : French dressing, please.

Dialog 3

A : Are you ready to order now?

B : I guess so. I just want something light. Do you have hamburgers?

A : Yes, Miss.

B : Good. Bring me a hamburger but hold the onions.

Dialog 4

A : May I help you, sir?
B : Yes, I think I'll have roast beef.
A : Will you have soup or juice?
B : I think I'd like tomato juice.
A : Can I get you anything to drink?
B : Coffee with the dessert, please.

Useful Expressions

1. This lunch is on me.
2. Which do you serve, table d'hôte or á la carte?
3. Pass me the salt, please.
4. I can't make up my mind.
5. This is not what I ordered.
6. Let's go Dutch.
7. Please give me a rain check.

Lunch is on me : 점심을 내가 사지. "내가 낼게!" 할 땐 'It's on me.'라면 된다. 'Let's go Dutch'하면 요금 각자부담하자는 뜻이다. 요금 각자 부담이란 말은 'Dutch treat'이다. Dutch pay란 말은 쓰지 않도록.
table d'hôte : 정식.
á la carte : 일품요리, 주문식단(주문하는 매 dish마다 요금별도 계산).

Unit 16 DINNER(Waiter/Waitress)

■A = Guest, ■B = Waiter

Dialog 1

A : What's good on the menu tonight?

B : We are selling a lot of flounder tonight. We have it baked or broiled.

A : I'm not too strong on fish. I'll just have a medium rare steak.

B : Yes, sir. Would you like baked potato or French fries?

A : Baked potato with sour cream, French dressing on my salad.

B : Yes, sir.

Dialog 2

A : What kind of soup do you have?

B : We have potato, onion gratin soup, and clam chowder.

A : Clam chowder for us, please.

B : What would you like to drink?

A : We'll have beer. Two bottles, please.

B : And what would you like for dessert?

flounder : 넙치(가자미류).

A : Do you have ice cream?

B : Yes, we have Banana, Chocolate, and Peach.

A : Banana, please.

B : Will that be all? Thank you, sir.

A : Check, please!

B : Thank you, sir.

A : Shall I pay here?

B : Please pay at the cashier.

A : O.K. Thank you.

■A = Assistant Manager, ■B = Guest

Dialog 3

A : Did you enjoy your dinner?

B : Oh, very much. Excellent. By the way, we have here one "Happy Birthday and One Anniversary" to celebrate. How much do you charge for the celebration service?

A : Well, we charge you two dollars per person. So, that will be 14 dollars in your party. Also we serve you with Fresh pineapples from Hawaii.

A : Now we're gonna sing "Happy Birthday and Happy Anniversary" to you. Everybody, clap hands, please. Now here we go!

B : Thank you so much for the beautiful party.

anniversary : 기념일.

■A = Guest, B = Waiter

Dialog 4

A : Is there a specialty of the house?

B : Yes, ma'am. It's "Bulgogi".

A : What is it?

B : It's barbecued beef, ma'am, prepared Korean style.

A : Do you serve it with rice?

B : Yes, ma'am. We also serve 'Kimchee' with it.

Useful Expressions

1. Do you have a reservation?
2. What do you recommend?
3. Salad comes with the steak dinner.
4. The same for me.
5. I'm sorry to have kept you waiting.
6. Do you serve only table d'hôte, or can I order á la carte?

gonna : going to를 줄여서 발음 또는 철자하며, want to는 'wanna'로 흔히 쓰인다.

Unit 17 BAR

■A = Guest, ■B = Cocktail Waitress

Dialog 1

A : Miss, please show me the wine list.
B : Very well, sir. Here you are, sir.
A : Thank you. Please bring me a martini.
B : Yes, sir. Would you like it dry?
A : Yes, extra dry, please.
B : Very well sir.

Dialog 2

B : What would you like to drink, sir?
A : Give me Tom Collins.
B : Very good, sir. With gin, or with vodka?
A : Please make it with gin.
B : Yes, sir.
C : Give me Scotch.
B : What brand?
C : White Horse, double.
B : Soda or water?
C : Just plain water with plenty of ice.
B : Have some potato chips.
C : Good. Give me another. What's that bottle over there? Let me see it. Do you have a match?

B : Yes, sir.

C : You are pretty well stocked here.

B : Right, sir.

Dialog 3

A : What does "Scotch on the rocks" mean?

B : "Rocks" means ice. So it means straight Scotch with ice and no mixer.

A : I see. Are other things ordered that way, too?

B : Sure do. Bourbon on the rocks. Gin on the rocks. Martini on the rocks. And Vermouth on the rocks. There're lots of possibilities.

A : If you don't want anything in your liquor, what should you ask for?

B : Just say, "I'll have straight Scotch," or "Two straight whiskies, please."

■A = Bartender, ■B = uuest

Dialog 4

A : Would you care for anything to drink, sir?

B : Give Scotch and water.

A : Certainly, sir. What brand of Scotch would you like, sir?

B : Give me something with a fairly low proof.

A : Yes, sir. Would you like something else?

B : Give me coffee.

A : We are very sorry, sir. We cannot serve coffee here. Would you mind having orange juice or a lemon squash instead?

B : I haven't eaten yet. What would you recommend?

A : Well, let me see. I'd recommend Sherry, Vermouth, Martini, or Manhattan.

B : Please make this one a little sweeter.

Useful Expressions

1. Show me the wine list.
2. You are pretty well stocked here.
3. I'm still waiting for my drink.
4. I didn't order another drink.
5. This is on the house.
6. What kind of beer would you like to have?

"This is on the house."하면 식당 등에서 무료로 주는 dish 등을 말한다. 안주(side dish) 등. 앞에서도 언급했지만 공짜를 service란 말로 표현하면 안된다. p. 63참조.

Unit 18

ROOM SERVICE

■A = Room Service, ■B = Guest

Dialog 1

A : Room Service. May I help you, sir?

B : I want to have breakfast tomorrow morning.

A : What would you like to have, sir?

B : Well...! think I'll have tomato juice, two eggs sunny side-up, buttered toast, and coffee. And a sliced pineapple, please.

A : What time would you like it served, sir?

B : At seven. Is that O.K.?

A : Certainly, sir.

Dialog 2

A : Good evening, sir. May I help you?

B : Yes, I want dinner in my room. Let's see, I'll try the T-bone steak. Do you have vegetable soup?

A : Yes, we do.

B : Okay, bring me vegetable soup, steak, a combination salad and some coffee.

A : Thank you sir. May I have your name and room number, please.

B : Mr. Baker, room 1825.

Dialog 3

A : Good morning, room service. May I help you?

B : Hello, we want to have a continental breakfast for two.

A : Very well, sir. Which juice would you like? Tomato or orange.

B : One orange, please.

A : All right sir, coffee or tea?

B : Bring us coffee, please.

A : Very well, sir. May I have your name and room number, please?

B : This is Mr. Miller in room 1170.

A : Mr. Miller, 1170, We'll send your breakfast right away, sir. Thank you very much.

Useful Expressions

1. What would you like to have, sir?
2. What time would you like it served?
3. Good evening, room service clerk, sir.
4. Can I order right now?
5. May I have your room number, please?

Unit 19 USEFUL EXPRESSIONS

1. I'd like to make a reservation at your hotel.
2. Your hotel was recommended to me by the American Express.
3. Can you recommend me a hotel in the city?
4. Is there any Y.M.C.A. hotel in this town?
5. Don't you have any vacant rooms?
6. Haven't you got any cheaper room?
7. We have a lot of vacant rooms.
8. I'm sorry, sir. We're filled up.
9. Do you expect to stay here for some time?
10. Sorry, but we have no such discount arrangement.
11. The room is just in a mess.
12. Give the bed and room a good airing.
13. Something is wrong with the television set.
14. The phone is out of order.
15. You have a visitor at the desk.
16. What time would you have your breakfast?

17. May I make your bed now?

18. The curio shop is in the annex.

19. Is this laundry ready to go?

20. A button is missing. Have it fixed?

21. How about being our alarm clock?

22. How long does it take to get to the airport from here by city bus?

23. I want to place a long distance call to Philadelphia.

24. I'd like to make a reservation at your hotel.

25. Can I get the call through right away?

26. I'm sorry to disturb you.

27. Who is going to pay for all this?

28. The manager's line is busy.

29. Who's calling, please?

30. I want to speak to Mr. Brown.

31. I'll try to locate him.

32. Did you hurt yourself?

33. I used to be a boy myself.

34. I'll inform the maintenance department and the housekeeper.

35. Mr. Morton is not in his office right now.

36. What have you got this morning?

37. I'd like my bacon good and crisp.

38. I'm glad you liked it.

39. I'm sorry, spaghetti is not on the menu.

40. What kind of sauce would you like?

41. This lunch is on me.

42. Just anything will do.

43. What have you got in mind? What do you have in mind?

44. Tell me what's good on the menu today.

45. How about trying our boiled lobster with tartar sauce.

46. Please hurry the orders, won't you?

47. What's happened to my order?

48. I'm checking out. Will you make out my bill?

49. We hope you enjoyed your stay with us.

50. When can you get in touch with me?

51. How long do you expect to stay?

52. Would you like to vacate the room now?

53. We have your coupons, but they do not include service charges and taxes.

54. We'll have your statement ready in the morning.

55. Let me figure it out.

56. I'd like the money in local currency instead of dollars.

57. His bar bill alone was more than my monthly salary.

58. It is my pleasure to welcome you to our hotel.

59. If there is anything you want, please call me.

60. I'm very sorry, but it is against regulations of the hotel to allow dogs in the room.

61. I came to offer you the services of our hotel.

62. It's our business to give you quick service, Mr. York.

63. Your people will enjoy not only the luxuries of our hotel but the location as well.

64. Arranging convention is out of my line.

65. If your price is right, you have my approval.

66. What about having a cocktail this evening when you have finished?

67. Is it OK with you to put this up by the elevators?

'What have you got in mind?'나 **'What do you have in mind?'**는 머리에 떠오르는 뾰족한 수가 있습니까?('무슨 착상이 있느냐?'하고 물을 때 쓰는 표현). 이의 부정 응답으로는 I don't have any idea at all.
get in touch with~ : ~와 접촉을 갖다., …연락을 취하다.
(Ex. How can I get in touch with you?).
keep in touch with~ : 지금까지 가져온 접촉(관계)을 계속 유지하다.

- 당신이 Hilton Hotel의 예약부에 근무하는 직원일 때 외부 전화가 왔다. 즉시 전화응답을 한다면?
- Good afternoon?
- Hilton Hotel.
- Reservation, Miss Kim speaking.
- Can I help you?

- 호텔에는 여러 가지 편리한 service가 있는데 방마다 시설이나 service 이용 pamphlet을 잘 읽고 이용하라. 또한 호텔의 정관 check-out time 등도 유인물로 되어 있다.
- Room Service : 식사나 음료수를 주문하여 객실로 날라 달라고 하면 되는데 요금이 비교적 비싸고 (expensive)운반해온 Boy나 maid에게 약간의 tip을 잊어선 안된다.
- Laundry Service : 세탁물은 방에 비치된 자루에 넣어서 room maid에게 주면 된다.
- Morning Call : 전날 교환이나 front에 기상시간을 부탁하면 그 시간에 bell을 울려 깨워 준다.
- 'Don't disturb'라고 쓴 쪽지를 문 밖에 걸어 두면 늦도록 잠을 푹 잘 수 있다.

PART III
TOUR GUIDE

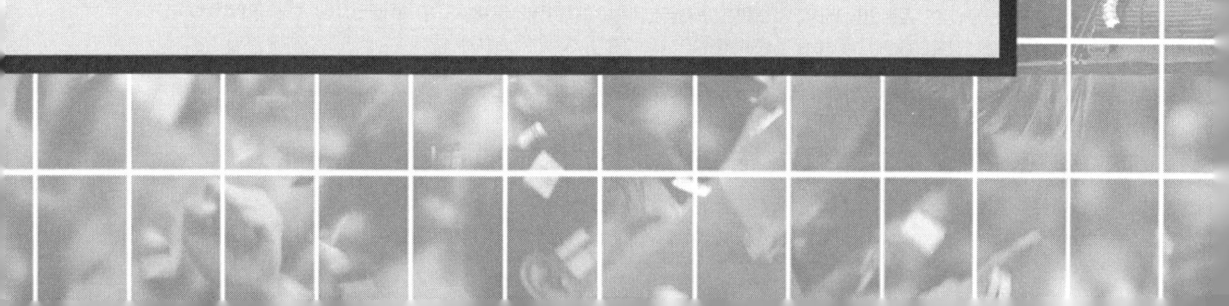

Personal Services as an Escort

A good escort should be sensitive to the needs of the group, to help form a sense of camaraderie and wellbeing.

The following are ten "dos and don'ts" :

Do

1. Smile -- everyone enjoys it's warmth and it is contagious.
2. Dress appropriately and be immaculately groomed at all times. It helps to reinforce your professionalism and the needed authority over the group.
3. Be patient. Traveling can be a very difficult adventure to the uninitiated.
4. Be prepared to have things go wrong-- with a little common sense and patience everything can be overcome.
5. Be friendly, courteous, calm, and, most of all, positive.
6. Be prepared-- research the destinations, hotels, etc.
7. Study the group so as to gear the trip around their interests.
8. Protect the sightseeing guides and bus drivers if their tips are not included in the package price by reminding the participants of this facts.
9. Learn the names of each tour participant.
10. Be understanding but firm regarding rules, etc.

Don't

1. Forget they are on vacation-- you are on the job !
2. Play favorites -- try to appear to like them all equally.
3. Develop emotional attachments.
4. Be patronizing or flippant.
5. Talk too much or feel you have to be the center of attention.
6. Recommend stores or restaurants unless you are asked.
7. Inform them of possible problems beforehand if there is nothing they can do about them anyway. The problem might not materialize and there is no need to upset the group for nothing.
8. Lie if you do not know something; admit it and find the answer.
9. Be late for anything.
10. Drink too much.

Unit 1 AT THE TRAVEL BUREAU

■A = Guest, ■B = Clerk

Dialog 1

A : I want to travel to Hong Kong by air.

B : Yes. When do you wish to go?

A : Next Friday, please.

B : Yes, sir... Do you want to travel by the economy class or first class, sir?

A : How much is it by the economy class?

B : 350 dollars ($350.00).

A : Could you tell me the time of the flight, please?

B : There's a flight leaving here at 11:55 a.m. on Wednesday, arriving in Hong Kong at 13:20.

A : Is it a jet plane?

B : Yes, it is, sir.

A : That sounds fine. I'd like to book a seat on the plane.

B : Yes, sir. I'll telephone the airline and ask for a reservation, and I'll leave a note in your box.

A : Thank you very much.

Dialog 2

A : Good morning.

B : Good morning, sir. Can I help you?

A : Do you arrange sightseeing tours of the city?

B : Yes, there's a tour every afternoon, sir, leaving here at two o'clock. The price is 10,000 won. I'm sure you'd find it very enjoyable.

A : Then I'll book two seats for this afternoon.

B : Yes, sir. That will be 20,000 won.

A : Thanks a lot.

Dialog 3

A : Good evening. May I help you, sir?

B : I'd like to go to London. What type of flight do you have?

A : We have all kinds of flights. What day would you like to leave?

B : Well, I'd like to leave on May 1st.

A : Would you like to go on first class or economy class?

B : Economy class, please.

I'm sure you'd find it very enjoyable : '무척 즐거우실 겁니다.'란 표현이고, 간단히 You should enjoy it. 또는 You should enjoy there.라는 좋은 표현이 있다.

Useful Expressions

1. When do you wish to go?
2. Do you want to travel by the economy class?
3. How much is it by the economy class?
4. Could you tell me the time of the flight?
5. There's a flight leaving here at seven sharp.
6. Do you arrange sightseeing tours of the city?

at seven sharp : 7시 정각에.

Unit 2 INFORMATIONS FOR TOUR

■A = Tourist, ■B = Clerk

Dialog 1

A : Where can I get a map of the subway lines?

B : Here's one for you, sir.

A : How much is it?

B : It's free of charge, sir. Compliments of the hotel. Everybody can have one of each.

A : My wife and I want to hire English-speaking guide for today.

B : Very well, sir. Please fill in this form.

A : What time will the guide come here?

B : Could you wait for an hour or two?

A : Sure.

Dialog 2

A : I'd like to take a look around the city this evening. Can I get a ticket for the sightseeing bus?

B : I'm sure you can, sir.

A : What night tours do they have?

B : They have many, sir. Just take "This Week in Seoul" with you, and choose the tour you'd like best.

A : Oh, thank you. I'd like to take tour.

B : Where can I catch the bus?

A : Take the bus in front of this hotel.

B : Thanks a lot.

■A = Tourist, ■B = Policeman, ■C = Passer-by

Dialog 3

A : Pardon me, can you tell me how to get to the Pagoda Park?

C : I'm sorry, I'm a stranger around here. That policeman will be able to help you.

A : May I ask you the way to Pagoda Park?

B : You'd better take the bus. Get on bus No. 134 or No. 37 at the bus stop over there.

A : How long will it take?

B : I guess it will take about 15 minutes. It's quite a few blocks from here.

A : Thanks a lot.

B : You are welcome.

Useful Expressions

1. Excuse me, but could you tell me the way to the Y.M.C.A.?
2. Can I get a ticket for the sightseeing bus?
3. Can I get a guide map of this city?
4. I want to hire an English-speaking guide today.
5. I'd like to take a look around the city this evening.
6. It'll take about fifty minutes at this time of day.

at this time of / day : 하루 중 /이맘때쯤에는
/ week : 일주일 중/
/ month : 한달 중/
어떤 교통수단을 이용할 때 유의할 점은 출·퇴근 시간의 혼잡할 때 즉 rush hour(영국영어에서는 흔히 peak hour) 때에는 시간이 훨씬 많이 소요된다는 것을 계산에 넣어야 한다는 것이다.

Unit 3 ON THE STREET

■A = Tourist, ■B = Passer-by

Dialog 1

A : Excuse me, but could you please tell me the way to the American Embassy?

B : Go down this street and turn to the left at the second corner, please.

A : How long will it take me to get there?

B : It's about 5 minutes' walk.

A : Thank you very much.

B : Not at all. You can't miss it.

■A = Tourist, ■B = Driver

Dialog 2

A : Hey, cab!

B : Where to, sir?

A : I'd like to go to Chosun Hotel.

B : Yes, sir. Is this your first visit here?

A : Yes, I've long been looking forward to coming to Korea.

B : Excuse me, but may I ask where you are from?

A : Chicago, U.S.A.

B : I see.

A : What's the name of this bridge that we're entering?

B : It's the Banpo-Bridge of the Han River. Now, we're in Seoul. What do you think of it?

A : Very beautiful city, I think.

B : Here we are. You may get off here, sir.

A : Thank you. Nice to talk to you. How much do I owe you?

B : ₩11,000, please.

A : Here you are. Keep the change.

B : Thank you, sir. I hope you'll enjoy your stay in Korea.

A : Thank you. I'm sure I will.

▪A = Tourist, ▪B = Passer-by

Dialog 3

A : Excuse me, sir.

B : May I help you?

A : How can I get to the pharmacy?

B : Go straight three blocks and turn left. It's on the second block on your right.

A : Go straight and turn left at the third block, right?

What do you think of Seoul : '서울의 인상이 어떻습니까?'라고 묻는 표현으로, How would you like Seoul? 또는 How did you find in Seoul?이라는 좋은 표현들이 있다.
look forward to …ing : ~을 학수고대하다. (eg : I'm looking forward to seeing you in the very near future.)

B : And there's a big flower shop on the corner.

B : Next to the shop is the pharmacy.

A : Thank you, sir. Is it far from here?

B : It's ten minutes' walk.

Useful Expressions

1. I'm a stranger around here.
2. It's about 3 blocks from here.
3. Where is this bus bound for?
4. Will this bus take me to Seoul Station?
5. What's the fare to Chongryang-ree?
6. Can I get off in front of Pagoda Park?

거리에서 외국인을 만났을 때 부드럽게 이어가는 대화의 예를 들어보면 :
A : Where are you from?
B : I'm from Boston, the United States.
A : How long have you been here?
B : I've been here for two weeks.
A : What do you think of Korea?(or How did you find in Korea?)
B : Oh, It's a beautiful country.

Unit 4

ON THE TRAIN

▪A = Mr. Kim, ▪B = Mr. Golden

Dialog 1

A : Do you like traveling on a train?

B : Yes, I like it very much.

A : Have you ever taken a long journey by train?

B : Yes, I once traveled from New York to Seattle.

A : How long did it take you to do the journey?

B : Nearly three days and nights. That was on the streamliner. It takes longer on regular trains.

A : What kind of trains are there?

B : The streamliners are diesel driven. Most of the trains are run by diesel, though. Electrically driven trains are used in the high mountains and on local runs around the suburbs of the big cities.

A : Are the American train cars like the Korean?

B : In construction, yes, what we call a day coach is similar. But, due to the long trip, many of the coaches have reclining seats which are very comfortable for sleeping.

Dialog 2

A : Are there other types of cars?
B : Yes, the sleeping car which we call a Pullman.
A : Are American trains always on time?
B : In winter they are often slowed down by snow, and in general not as punctual as they should be.
A : What classes are there on your trains?
B : Usually just two, Pullman and day coach.
A : Who's the man that checks the ticket?
B : He is the conductor. There are also an engineer who runs the train and porters who help you with your baggage.

Dialog 3

A : Excuse me, but is this Seat No. 88?
B : Yes, right here.
A : Thank you.
B : How far are you going?
A : As far as Kyongju.
B : Oh, are you? That's where I'm going, too.
A : That's good. I'm glad to meet you.
B : Are you going to do the sights of Kyongju?
A : Yes, I'd like to see Pusan, too.
B : How long are you going to stay in Kyongju?
A : About a week. My name is Thomas Brown. And you?
B : My name is Kim, Mee Son, Kim is my surname.

pullman : sleeping car on a railway train with comfortable chairs.

Useful Expressions

1. That's where I'm going, too.
2. How far are you going? (=Where are you heading?)
3. I am going as far as Kyongju.
4. Take subway and transfer at Kuro Station, and 5th stop from there.
5. Take No. 123 bus from the front of our hotel, and get off at the third stop.

That's where I'm going, too. : '저도 거기까지 가는데요.'라는 표현인데, 'You're in the same train.'하면 '동행이군요.' 하는 멋진 표현이 된다. 선박에서는 You're in the same boat. 버스에서는 You're in the same bus.라고 하면 된다.

Unit 5 AT THE BANK

■A = Tourist, ■B = Information Clerk

Dialog 1

A : Where can I cash some traveler's checks?

B : Please go to the third window.

A : Thank you.

B : You're welcome.

■A = Tourist, ■B = Teller

Dialog 2

A : Would you cash this $50 check, please?

B : Certainly. How would you like it?

A : Well, I'd like one twenty, two tens, one five, and five ones.

B : All right, sir. Here you are. Twenty, thirty, forty, forty-five, forty-six, forty-seven. forty-eight, forty-nine, and fifty. Would you check it, please?

A : Yes, I'd like to.

B : Thank you, sir.

traveler's check : 여행자 수표.
cash : 현찰(n), 현찰로 바꾸다.(v)
When can I cash this traveler's check?
여행자 수표를 어디서 현찰로 바꿀 수 있나요?

Dialog 3

A : Could you exchange these American dollars into Korean money?

B : Yes, sir. How much do you have?

A : $54.75.

B : All right.

A : What is the current exchange rate ?

B : One dollar equals 1,200 won.

A : It has changed, hasn't it?

B : Yes, it has. The American dollar is still going up.

A : Is that right? That's good for me.

B : Here it is, 64,847 won, sir.

A : Well, I think there is a mistake in your calculations.

B : What? Oh, sorry. I have to pay you 50 more won.

A : Right. That is correct.

B : Thank you, sir.

A : Thanks.

Useful Expressions

1. Please sign your name, sir.
2. Would you cash this $100 check, please?
3. How would you like it?
4. One American dollar equals 1,200 Korean won.
5. We are not authorized to accept them.

exchange rate : 환율.
One dollar equals 1,200 won : 1달러는 1,200원에 해당됩니다.

Unit 6 AT THE TRAVEL AGENCY

■A = Tourist. ■B = Clerk

Dialog 1

A : I was thinking of going to Europe. What type of flight do you have?

B : Where would you like to go?

A : I'd like to go to Paris. I was thinking of staying in Paris for a while.

B : We have all kinds of flights. What day would you like to leave?

A : Well, I'd like to leave on March 20th, if I can.

Dialog 2

B : Would you like to go on first class or economy class?

A : I'd like to go on economy, of course.

B : O.K. I'll check it. Well, there isn't any on economy.

A : Oh, yeah?

B : I recommend going by Northwest Orient flight. This one is not too expensive.

A : Do you know if a seat is available?

B : Yes, there is.

A : O.K. I'll take this flight then.

Useful Expressions

1. I'd like to go on economy class.
2. Do you know if a seat is available?
3. I'll take this flight then.
4. Thank you for calling, sir.
5. Your reservation number is 707.

Unit 7 AT THE DEPARTMENT STORE

■A = Sales Girl. ■B = Tourist

Dialog 1

A : May I help you?
B : Yes, please show me that doll.
A : This one?
B : Yes.
A : This will make a good souvenir.
B : What is this made of?
A : The head is made of stainless steel and the body is made of wood.
B : It is really interesting. How much is it?
A : Five thousand won, sir.

Dialog 2

B : How much is that bigger one?
A : Ten thousand won, sir.
B : Well, ten thousand won. That's a little expensive for me. Would you make it cheaper?
A : I'm afraid not, but if you take two dolls....
B : No, I don't want two.
A : Then, I can't.

souvenir : something taken, bought or received as a gift, and kept as a reminder of a person, place or event.

B : Well, O.K. I'll take that small one.

A : All right, sir. Five thousand won, please.

■A = Tourist, ■B = Information Girl

Dialog 3

A : Excuse me. Where is the men's clothing section?

B : 4th floor, sir.

A : I see, but it is too crowded.

B : Well, then why don't you take the escalator?

A : Yes, but I don't know where it is.

B : Well, you have to go all the way down there and turn to the right.

A : Thank you so much. Oh, one more thing. Is there a women's clothing section there, too?

B : No, sir. There is one on the second floor in the new building.

A : Can I go there from here straight?

B : Yes, you can.

A : And you have a food section in the basement, right?

B : I'm sorry, we don't.

A : Oh, yeah. Well, O.K. Thank you very much.

Useful Expressions

1. I want to buy a souvenir.

2. I'll take that small one.

3. Where can I buy a watch?

4. I'm just looking.
   Can I have a look?

5. May I help you, sir? What can I help you?

Unit 8 TALKING ABOUT SIGHTSEEING

■A = Mr. Chang, ■B = Mr. Baker

Dialog 1

A : What kind of places would you like to visit?

B : I'd like to see Korean things around Seoul and Chéju-Island.

A : Then, Chéju-Island and Seorak Mountain are the best places.

B : Is that right? I want to see Chéju-Island, too.

A : By the way, Thomas, what are you going to do tomorrow?

B : I'd like to do the sights of Seoul.

A : I'll show you around Seoul, then.

B : That's very kind of you.

A : The pleasure is mine. Well, have you ever travelled by ship?

B : Never. I've seen it in a Korea guide book.

Dialog 2

A : Oh, it's nine o'clock already. I'm afraid I've stayed too late.

B : Do you have to go so soon?

A : Thank you very much for the pleasant evening.

B : You're welcome. We had a good time, too.

B : Must you go already?

A : Yes, thank you very much for inviting me.

B : Please come and see us again soon.

A : Thank you, I will see you tomorrow. Good night, Mr. Kim.

B : Good night, John.

Useful Expressions

1. What kind of places would you like to visit?
2. I'd like to see things about Korea.
3. What are you going to do tomorrow?
4. I'd like to do the sights of Seoul.
5. I'll show you around Seoul.

'I'm afraid I've stayed too long?' : '너무 오래 머물러 있어 죄송하군요.' 하는 표현. 이와 다소 다른 것으로, 'I'm afraid I wear out my welcome.' '너무 자주 드나들어 성가시죠?'하는 아주 고상한 표현도 있다.

Unit 9 DOWNTOWN SEOUL (I)

■A = Guide, ■B = John Smith

Dialog 1

A : It's a fine day, isn't it?

B : Yes, very nice.

A : I'll act as a guide today, John. What would you like to see first?

B : I'd like to go up to Mt. Nam-san.

A : That's a good idea. I'll take you there.

B : What's the tower on the top?

A : Oh, it's Nam-san Tower.

B : How high is it?

A : Well, about 500 feet high.

Dialog 2

A : We're at the crest of the mountain. Here's a field glass.

B : Just look down there. That building is the Kyông-bok Palace, isn't it?

A : You're right. Well, how can you find it?

B : In the guidemap.

A : It's Kyông-bok Palace. Where's the National Assembly Building, do you know?

B : That's the National Assembly Building in Yoeui-do, isn't it? I've seen it in the guidebook.

Dialog 3

A : Finally here we are. The building you see over there is the City Hall of Seoul.

B : Oh, I see. What's that stone wall?

A : It's Tôksoo Palace. That's one of the places worth visiting in Seoul, I think.

B : Would you take me there?

A : Yes, I will. Come with me. Here we are in the Plaza.

B : These are fine grasses here and there, aren't they?

A : Here's the best place for many people and artists. Look! They are displaying an art exhibition.

B : It's a lovely place. What a graceful building it is!

A : How about going and seeing another place, if you want?

B : That's good. Well, where to?

A : I'll show you bronze statues in Sejong-no and Kwanghwa-moon. All right?

B : Are you going there, now? It's good. Show me the way.

Useful Expressions

1. Where are we now?
2. That's one of the places worth visiting in Seoul.
3. They are displaying an art exhibition.
4. What a graceful building it is!
5. Show me the way to Sejong-no.

Unit 10 DOWNTOWN SEOUL (II)

■A = Guide, ■B = John Smith

Dialog 1

A : That's the bronze statue of Lee, Soon Shin, a great warrior of the Yi Dynasty.

B : Oh, I see. Is that a famous "Turtle Ship", then? I mean that in front of him.

A : How did you know that? Why, certainly!

B : I've seen it in the guide book. It says Turtle Ship's story there. Is this the business center of Seoul?

Dialog 2

A : Now, here's Myông-dong. That's the best shopping district in Seoul

B : Is it? Certainly! Oh, how beautiful those flowers are!

A : They're roses. There are more than 100 varieties, I have. Well, you look a little tired now.

B : Anyway, let's finish here today. Did you enjoy?

A : Yes, sure. What a nice day today!

Dialog 3

A : That's the South Gate, and we call it Namdaemoon.

B : What a splendid building it is!

A : It's National Treasure No. 1 in Korea. Watch your step! There are men working around it.

B : This poster says "For Subway," I know.

A : It's the third line.

B : What's that classic building?

A : Classic? Oh, that's Seoul Station. It's too old.

B : What's the name of this street?

A : This street is in front of South Gate Market.

Useful Expressions

1. What a splendid building it is!
2. It's National Treasure No. 1 in Korea.
3. It was built after the Korean War.
4. This is the best shopping district in Seoul.
5. There are more than 100 varieties.

Unit 11 TICKETING TO SOKCH'O

■A = Tourist, ■B = Agent

Dialog 1

A : I'd like to go to Sokch'o tomorrow morning. Give me two tickets, please. Round trip, I need.

B : Beg your parden?

A : Two tickets to Sokch'o.

B : You've got the wrong place. We have no express bus to Sokch'o. You'd better go and get it at Kangnam Terminal.

Dialog 2

A : What's the fare to Sokch'o?

B : Forty five hundred and ten won, please.

A : You mean round trip or one way trip?

B : We've not round trip. One way only. Well today's over. Would you have tomorrow's?

A : Yes, two tickets, please.

B : Here are your tickets.

Dialog 3

A : What time is the bus for Sokch'o leaving this terminal?

B : The bus starts every 20 minutes all day.

A : Is it a long ride to Sokch'o?

B : Yes, it'll take about five hours. Is it your first visit to Korea?

A : Yes, I arrived here only five days ago.

B : Have a nice trip.

Useful Expressions

1. What's the fare to Sokcho?
2. We have no round trip (ticket).
3. Today's over.
4. Is it a long ride to Sokch'o?
5. I arrived here only five days ago.

Unit 12 BUS TRAVEL TO MT. SEORAK

▪A = Tourist, ▪B = Guide

Dialog 1

A : Our bus is leaving in a few minutes, isn't it?

B : Right. Do you have tickets with you?

A : Of course, two tickets. One for me, and one for you. Here, take this ticket.

B : Thank you for your trouble.

A : No, problem.

B : Here comes the bus!

A : Is this the right bus for Sokcho?

B : Look! It says "For Sokcho." Let's take it.

Dialog 2

Announcement: "Good morning ladies and gentlemen! We wish to welcome you aboard this bus. We've just left Kangnam Terminal and are now en route to Kangnung, Daegwalyong, as far as Sokcho. We expect to arrive at Sokcho Terminal at 2 p.m. We wish you enjoy your trip. Thank you."

A : I feel like a carsick. Are you all right?

B : Did you suffer from carsick?

A : Yes, sometimes. Have you any medicine good for carsickness?

B : Here it is. Some sleep, that'll do you good.

A : Look! There, many farms, here and there.

B : Yes, many.

A : What would you have, tea or coffee?

B : Tea, please.

A : I'll have coffee, please.

B : It's a fine day, isn't it?

■A = Guide, ■B = Tourist

Dialog 3

Announcement: "Ladies and gentlemen, we'll be arriving at Sokch'o Terminal very soon. Attention, please. Remain seated until the bus has come to a standstill. We hope you've enjoyed your trip, and that you will take with us again. Thank you."

A : We are in Sokcho finally. Did you enjoy your trip?

B : Sure. I did.

A : Is that right. I'm glad to hear that.

come to standstill : 완전히 정차하다. 라는 표현 흔히 'Come too a complete stop'이라고 한다.

Useful Expressions

1. We are now en route to Daegwalyong.
2. I feel like carsick.
3. Do you have any medicine good for carsickness?
4. Yes, we have some pills for airsickness.
5. We will be arriving at Sokch'o Terminal very soon.
6. I hope you will take with us again.
7. Ladies and gentlemen! Please remain seated until the plane has come to a complete stop.

Unit 13 MT. SEORAK

■A = Guide, ■B = Tourist

Dialog 1

A : This is the National Park, Mt. Seorak. There are many tourist attractions.

B : How nice! Will you take me there now?

A : Of course.

B : Oh, what a wonderful waterfall!

A : It's indeed a magnificent sight.

B : How high is that?

A : It's at least 120 feet high.

B : Is that right? Well, what do you call this waterfall?

A : We call it "Biryong".

B : What do you mean by "Biryong?"

A : It means "Flying-Dragon."

The weather is too beautiful, I feel as if I were in Eden.

A : Right! Me, too.

■A = Tourist, ■B = Guide

Dialog 2

A : Now, where are you going to take me? What's the next course?

B : Let's call it a day. You look tired, aren't you?

A : I think so. And you?

B : Me, too. How about going to the hotel and taking a rest?

A : That's a good idea. Oh, look! The slope road is coming in sight. And the air is getting more and more refreshing, isn't it?

B : Yes, this is over 3,000 feet above sea level.

Dialog 3

A : What's the name of that high peak?

B : It's Taechong Peak, top of Mt. Seorak.

A : Sure? How high is it?

B : It's over 1,700m above sea level. Now, let's go to downtown.

A : Yes, Mr. Kim.

Let's call it a day : '오늘은 그만 합시다.' 라는 표현
Let's make it definitely for Monday : 그 일은 월요일로 확정합시다.

Useful Expressions

1. Will you take me there up to the hill?

2. Let's come and see over the ridge.

3. I'm worn out.

4. What a wonderful waterfall!

5. It's a magnificent sight.

6. What do you mean by that?

7. It's quite another sight.

- I'm worn out. 나는 피로하다./지쳤다.
- "Please, give me a raincheck!"에서 raincheck란 말의 의미를 모를 땐, "What do you mean by 'raincheck'?"라고 하면 상대방이 설명해 줄 것이다.
- 철자를 모를 땐, "How do you spell?"또는 "Would you spell that for me?"

Unit 14 KYÔNGJU AREA

■A = Guide. ■B = Tourist

Dialog 1

A : Is this your first visit to Kyôngju?

B : Yes, that's right, Mr. Kim. I'm so happy that you're going to be my guide. Isn't Kyôngju your hometown?

A : Yes, I know my way around pretty well.

B : What do you recommend for me to see in Kyôngju?

A : Kyôngju is the home of old Korean fine arts and so you can see many kinds of ancient treasures. You should enjoy here.

B : I imagine that the ancient temples are the most outstanding features of this old capital.

A : Yes, they all offer much in the way of historical interest.

Dialog 2

A : Here we are at Pulguk-sa Temple. Isn't the view from here simply breathtaking?

B : It certainly is. I never expected to find such a magnificent temple in the middle of this mountain.

B : Is Sokuram really a cave?

A : Yes. In the center of the cave we can find a large image of Buddha more than five meters high. On the wall, there are beautiful and lively images of Buddha and the Giant.

B : After we have taken in Sokuram, will we see all the places of importance?

A : It's impossible to see everything in such a short time.

B : Why does Kyôngju have so many historical attractions?

A : Because Kyôngju had been the capital of the Shilla Dynasty for more than ten centuries.

Dialog 3

A : This is the famous Pulguk-sa Temple.

B : It's a very interesting place, isn't it? Well, this stone is too heavy to lift. How did they build?

A : It's a surprise to me, too. I have no idea. Let's go inside.

B : That's the house of worship, isn't it? What a huge wooden building!

A : Yes, it's quite symmetrical and beautiful. Here's Taewungjôn, what we call.

B : Look at those lotus blossoms. How beautiful they are!

A : The Pulguk-sa Temple is also famous for its beautiful gardens and ponds.

B : Are there many temples in this area?

A : Yes, more than fifty.

B : A lot of temples!

A : Sure. And famous museum, and many old mounds. How about Kyôngju?

B : This view alone is indeed worth coming all the way to Korea to see.

A : I'm glad to hear that.

Useful Expressions

1. Is this your first visit to Kyôngju?

2. Kyôngju was the capital of the Shilla Dynasty.

3. Kyôngju is the home of old Korean fine arts.

4. The ancient temples are the most outstanding features of this old capital.

5. Isn't the view from here simply breathtaking?

Unit 15

CHEJU AREA

▪A = Tourist, ▪B = Guide

Dialog 1

A : Oh! What a big waterfall! Have you seen like that?

B : No, I haven't. It's Chônjeyon Falls, I hear.

A : Do you remember Niagara Falls?

B : Yes, I've got a very fine tour. How high is it?

A : Well, I can't remember it.

B : What do you think about 'Nature?'

A : Nature? I love it. Nature is life, and life is real.

B : Certainly! As the golden saying goes, "God made the country, and men made the town," you know.

Dialog 2

A : Why! How did you know that golden saying, Mr. Kim?

B : I read it in a book. Haven't you ever heard of Yongdu-am?

'God made the country, and made the town.'이라고 하는 말은 인간이 아무리 애써도 자연만큼 아름다움을 창조해 내진 못한다는 말. 얼마나 인간이 무기력한가! Nature never betrays the heart that loves her(W. B. Yeats).

A : I've never heard of it. What's it famous for?

B : It's a rock. It's a dragon head, I mean. The rock looks like a dragon's head.

A : You mean Dragon Peak?

B : Right! By the way, how did you know it?

A : Nothing. I read it in a guide book.

Dialog 3

A : We must take lots of pictures.

B : Cheju has some of the most beautiful women in Korea.

A : Where's your camera?

B : Here, I have it. How about having lunch?

A : Let's go and eat.

B : Let's have something special.

■A = Guide, ■B = Tourist, ■C = Driver

Dialog 4

A : We've arrived in Cheju, at last. Well, where shall we go first?

B : Look at the sea-bed. It's so clear and blue.

A : Certainly it is! You can see clearly the bottom.

B : It's like an island country, isn't it? We must take lots of pictures.

A : Cheju has some of the most beautiful women in Korea. Just look over there.

B : Here's a beautiful island, isn't it? Where's your camera?
A : Yes, I have. It's a perfect day for a sight, I think.
C : Where are you going, may I ask?
B : I'm gong to Sôgwipo, Chôngbang, and Chônjeyon Waterfall.
C : Is it your first visit here?
A : Right; Well... How did you know that?
C : I'm ready for whatever tourists want. I'll take you there, if you are all right.

Useful Expressions

1. Haven't you ever heard of Yongdu-am?
2. I've never heard of it.
3. He's the best driver, isn't he?
4. How about lunch?
5. Let's have something good.

Unit 16 USEFUL EXPRESSIONS

1. I've been here for two weeks.
2. How long have you been here?
3. I've been to New York.
4. Have you ever been to Honolulu?
5. Is this the right way to the Y.M.C.A.?
6. Turn to the right.
7. Just go straight on.
8. You can't miss it.
9. It will take about fifteen minutes on foot.
10. Turn left at the first crossing.
11. It's in that direction.
12. You've come too far.
13. Ask at the police station over there.
14. It's the third house from the corner.
15. It's on the left-hand side of the street.
16. It's on the other side of the railroad tracks.
17. I know where it is. I'll take you there.
18. You're in the wrong district.
19. You'd better ask that policeman.

20. Where can I take the bus to Sokcho?

21. You must get off at the next stop, and transfer to car No. 35.

22. Have small change ready, please.

23. How many more stops to Tongdaemoon-Gate?

24. This was delayed on account of traffic accident.

25. There are many coming right after this.

26. We've passed that point, but you have to go back 2 stops.

27. This ticket is good only for the day.

28. No transfer is issued.

29. Is this your first visit to Kyŏngju?

30. I'm happy that you're going to be my guide.

31. I know my way around pretty well.

32. Is this your first visit here in Korea?

33. Where are you from?

34. Do come in, please.

35. Did you have any difficulty in finding my house?

36. Did you have a good time?

37. Yes, I certainly had a good time.

38. I'm sorry to hear that.

39. Here's something for you.

40. Thanks a lot.

41. Is there any hospital near here?

42. Would you like a drink before your meal?

43. Pass me the salt and pepper, please.

44. Do you mind if I smoke?

45. Not at all. Go right ahead.

46. Go ahead, please.

47. Hold the line, please.

48. How have you been?

49. Did you enjoy your flight?

50. Say hello to your wife for me.

51. Would you come and see me when you're free?

52. Why don't you come to my house for dinner tomorrow?

53. Thank you, I'll be glad to.

54. We're forced to change our itinerary a little bit, that's why I'm calling you.

55. How do you want to change your itinerary?

약간의 tip을 줄 때, 'Here's something for you.'라는 부드러운 표현이 있다.
Say hello to A : A에게 안부전해주세요.
keep the change. 하면 "거스름돈을 챙겨 넣어요." 라고 거스름돈을 tip으로 주는 경우에 쓰이는 표현이다.
Say hello to John. John에게 안부 전해 주세요.

- **"Have you ever been here before."**는 전에 와 보신 적이 있습니까? 라는 표현으로서 Have+ever+p.p…?. 경험을 묻는 문장임은 다 아는 사실이나, American English 에서는 흔히 Did you ever+V…?로서 전자와 같은 의미의 구분으로 쓰고 있다
  EX : British English : Have you ever seen an emu?
  American English : did you ever see an emu?
  Ex. Did you ever feel like crying?
- You can't miss it. 틀림없이 찾으실 겁니다.

PART IV

OVERSEAS TOUR CONDUCTOR SERVICE

1 RECONFIRMATION OF RESERVATION
2 ON BOARDING
3 IMMIGRATION, QUARANTINE & CUSTOMS
4 MEETING SERVICE
5 CHECKING-IN THE HOTEL (I)
6 CHECKING-IN THE HOTEL (II)
7 RESERVATION FOR BREAKFAST
8 SIGHTSEEING ARRANGEMENTS
9 SIGHTSEEING
10 SHOPPING
11 PLANT VISIT
12 APPOINTMENT BY TELEPHONE
13 FOOD SERVICE
14 RENT-A-CAR
15 CHECKING-OUT
16 CHECKING-IN (AT THE AIRPORT)
17 USEFUL EXPRESSIONS

Unit 1

RECONFIRMATION OF RESERVATION

■A = Korean tour conductor, ■B = Airlines' agent

Dialog 1

A : Is this Northwest Orient Airlines? Group desk, please. We'll take Northwest Orient Airlines' flight 009 to New York this Saturday afternoon. We'd like to reconfirm reservations for our party of 32 people in all.

B : Did you make reservations when you purchased the air tickets?

A : Yes, that was done in Bangkok.

B : May I have the name of your group?

A : It's Korea Tour.

B : I don't see your name on the reservation list.

Dialog 2

A : It could be listed under "Korea Tour." Could you check it again, please?

B : Hold the line a minute. Yes, I have it now. Thirty-two seats are now confirmed on flight 009 to New York this Saturday afternoon. May I ask your local contact?

A : I'm at Hilton Hotel, with telephone number 212-6031, extension 1524. My name is Mr. Kim.

B : I see. The flight takes off at 4 p.m.

A : When do we have to check in at the airport.

B : 2:30 p.m. at the latest, please.

A : One more thing I want to ask you. Do you serve any meals in the flight?

B : Dinner and breakfast will be served.

Useful Expressions

1. May I speak to group desk?
2. Get me group desk, please.
3. Did you make reservations?
4. May I have the name of your group?
5. I'm the tour escort of Korea Tour.

Unit 2 ON BOARDING

■A = Korean tour conductor, ■B = Airlines' cabin attendant

Dialog 1

A : Good afternoon.
We are on a group movement with 32 people in all. We'd like to know where we sit. Two of us are non-smokers.

B : Good afternoon. Welcome aboard.
Can I see your boarding cards, please?

A : Seats for non-smokers are 1-A and B.
Yes, here you are.

B : Your seats are from 23-A through 27-F.
Please proceed about 12 rows aback.

A : Thank you.

B : Would you please tell your group to put their carry-on baggage under the seat, not on the overhead rack?

A : We have one bulky bag. Where do we put it?

B : We can keep it in the storage bins on this aircraft.

Dialog 2

A : By the way, we all have ED Cards. It's not necessary to give us any.

B : Are you a tour conductor of the Korean tour group? My name is Anne.

A : Glad to know you Miss Anne. Yes, I'm a tour escort and my name is Kim.

B : Where's your destination?

A : New York. Tell me later the stop-over places and time. I'll take orders for drinks of my group and let you know.

B : That's very kind of you, Mr. Kim. We'll stop over at Seattle for about two hours.

Dialog 3

A : Do you have any caffeine-free coffee?

B : Sorry, we have no caffeine-free coffee in our pantry.

A : We need more blankets. Do you have any extra ones?

B : Yes, we have some in the overhead rack. Now, do you need earphones? $2.50 for each.

A : We'll take them. $80 for 32 earphones, right?

B : Exactly.

caffeine-free coffee=decaffeinated coffee : 카페인이 함유되어 있지 않은 커피. 여기서 'free'란 없다는 의미. duty-free 면세의.

black coffee : cream(milk)을 타지 않은 커피. sugar를 탔는가 타지 않았는가 하고는 관계없다. 왜냐하면 Sugar doesn't make any difference in the color of coffee.

Useful Expressions

1. Can you tell me the local time in Seattle?
2. Will you show me some magazines or newspapers?
3. Give me a Scotch and water, please.
4. This seat isn't comfortable. Can you check it (for me)?
5. Could you turn the reading-lamp a little bit? I need to sleep.
6. One of our members feels like throwing up. Can you give him some antimotion sickness pills?
7. We are now flying at an altitude of 30,000 feet and at a ground speed of 580 miles per hour.
8. What's the actual flying time from Seoul to Seattle?

What's the local time in New York? : '뉴욕 현지 시각이 몇시냐'는 물음.
local time ~ : ~ 현지 시각.
actual flying time : 실제 비행시간.

Unit 3 IMMIGRATION, QUARANTINE, & CUSTOMS

■A = Korean tour conductor, ■B = An officer at the quarantine office

Dialog 1

B : Let me check your health card (shot record).

A : Yes, here it is.

B : Are you vaccinated against cholera?

A : No, no cholera shot was given.
We came from Korea.

B : Oh, I see. All right.
Now proceed to the passport check.

■A = Tour conductor, ■B = An officer at the passport control

Dialog 2

A : Where do we line up?

B : Right here. Are you the tour leader of this Korean group?

A : Yes, I am (a tour leader).

B : How long do you want to stay in America? (=How long do you intend to stay here?)

A : (We will be staying here) for 17 days.

B : Are you on a business trip or on a pleasure trip? What's the main purpose of your visit?

A : (We are on a) business trip.

B : Are you visiting any other countries.

A : No, (we are traveling in) America only.

B : Where are you going to tour?

A : Well, after 3 days in New York, we'll be visiting Chicago, Boston and Louisville.

B : Then, I'll give you 22 days. Will that be all right?

A : That will be fine, sir. Thank you.

▪A = Tour conductor, ▪B = Customs inspector

Dialog 3

A : We are a party of 32. I'm the tour escort. We have 32 bags in all.

B : All right, (do you have) anything to declare?

A : No, (we have) nothing to declare.

B : (Do you have) any liquor, cigarettes.
pearls and the like?

A : Each of us has less than two bottles of whisky, 100 cigarettes, but has not any pearls, precious metals or jewels.

출 · 입국 수속절차와 용어는 p. 16~18을 참조.

B : Very well, open this one and that one, please. What's this?

A : It's seaweed. It's a gift for a Korean friend who's been here for a long time.

B : What's that box?

A : It's a music box for his personal use.

B : What's that wrapped in the paper?

A : It's a piece of ginseng.

B : What's in the can?

A : Korean Kimchee.

B : And this?

A : That's some instant noodlcs. I'm going to cat it mysclf.

B : What's in the jar?

A : Pickled cucumber.

B : Is that the one that makes your mouth water?

A : Exactly.

B : All right. I'll check the rest of the bags with OK chalk marks. Bring the bags one at the time.

A : Thank you, sir.

Useful Expressions

1. Certificate, please.
2. Yes, here it is.
3. We're a party of forty-five.
4. I'm the tour escort of a Korean group.

5. Do you have anything to declare?

6. What's the main purpose of your visit?

7. We're going to make an observation tour of various companies.

8. Are you disembarkation passengers?

9. They're all our personal effects.

10. How many(people) are there in your party?

- **Transit passenger** : person traveling via an itinerary which includes one or more spot in foreign countries which are not the person's destination.
- **disembarkation passenger**↔transit passenger

Unit 4 MEETING SERVICE

■A = Tour conductor, ■B = Porter

Dialog 1

A : Please take these bags and put them on the bus.

B : How many bags do you have?

A : Thirty-two in all. They are the ones all with Korea Travel Service's yellow tags for identification.

B : May I have your claim tags?

A : Here they are. How many pieces of baggage do you count?

B : I count 31 so far. I couldn't find the 32nd.

A : The last one is that cardboard box by the counter. That'll make it 32.

B : Exactly. I see Korean characters on the box.

A : Please keep an eye on these bags, I'll check the bus. I'll be right back.

keep an eye on~ : ~을 봐주다(자리를 비운 사이).
identification : 동일하다는 증명(확인).
*신분증명서(주민등록증) : p. 173 참조.

■A = Tour conductor, ■B = Representative from local travel agent

Dialog 2

B : Excuse me, but are you Mr. Kim of Korea Tour? I'm David Smith from Gay Travel Agency.

A : Yes, I am. Nice meeting you, Mr. Smith.

B : Welcome to New York. I'm told you have 33 people. Are they all here?

A : We're one member less. We are all here 32 people including myself.

B : I see, then where can I see your bags?

A : They'll come out soon, all with yellow tags.

B : That's an excellent idea to handle bags.

A : Can I use the baggage truck?

B : Oh, no, you can't. Only skycaps may handle this.

Dialog 3

A : Can I have our voucher?

B : Yes, but not here. I'll pass it to you on the bus.

A : Great, thank you.

B : Are you all on board?

A : One of our members is now in the rest room. Hold the bus for a minute, please.

B : I see. Here is your voucher you told me (before). Also, you have here 32 copies of your tour itinerary.

A : Thanks a lot, Mr. Smith.

B : As you see batch of voucher has 23 coupons. Will you please check it?

A : Everything is fixed. No problem.

B : If you have any changes, fill out the reverse side (back side) of the coupon in detail and endorse it, please.

A : We are all here now. Shall we get started?

■A = Tour conductor, ■B = Porter, ■C = Bus line's staff

Dialog 4

B : Where can I see your bus?

A : The bus should be here. It's Boston Line's bus. Isn't that yellow one ours?

B : I don't think so. It's for another party.

A : I'm contact the bus line to see what happened. Where can I find a pay phone?

B : Go straight ahead this way. It's on the corner to the left. Have you got a dime? You need a dime for a city call.

A : I've got it. Hello, is this BOSTON Line? I want to talk to the dispatcher.

C : Dispatcher Brown speaking. May I help you?

A : This is the tour escort of Korea Tour. We are all here now at the airport waiting for your bus.

C : Please go ahead.

Dialog 5

A : I tried to find your bus, but no bus was found here. Why is there no bus?

C : I didn't know you were coming in on this early flight. You are expected to arrive by Northwest Flight 205 at 6 this evening.

A : It couldn't be, we are all here anyway. There must be something wrong on your side.

C : Now, I'll call the bus terminal to send a bus to the airport right away. Can you wait another hour?

A : We can't wait that long. Our members are very much upset. What do you say we cancel your bus and take a limousine bus to Youngs Terminal?

C : If you insist that way, I must agree to cancel the arrangement.

A : Call Hilton Hotel at 3 o'clock this afternoon. My name is Kim. Let us talk about the detail of this discrepancy at that time.

C : Very well, I'll call you at 3. Thank you for calling.

■A = Tour conductor, ■B = Limousine's driver

Dialog 6

A : Is this the limousine (bus) to Youngs Terminal?

B : Yes, it is. Are you traveling alone?

A : No, we are (traveling) on a group movement of 32 people with baggage.

B : Bring your bags right here, so that I may put them on the bus.

A : Skycaps will bring them here.

B : I see. Ten dollars per person to the terminal. You pay me now.

A : Here's 320 dollars for 32 people. Can you give me a receipt of that amount?

B : I'll work it out as soon as we arrive at the terminal and give it to you there.

A : Is the terminal very far from here?

B : No, not very far, say about 30 miles from here. It's about 30 minutes' ride.

A : Here comes the baggage. Will you load the bags on the bus?

B : (After 30 minutes) We are now approaching Youngs Terminal. Have a nice trip.

A : Thank you, we will.

Useful Expressions

1. How do you do, Mr. James? Nice to meet you.
2. Welcome to Chicago.
3. How was your flight?
4. Oh, it was wonderful.
5. Where is the bus parked?

Unit 5 CHECKING-IN

▪A = Tour conductor, ▪B = Doorperson, ▪C = Front desk clerk, ▪D = Bell captain, ▪E = Guest

Dialog 1

A : Please call porters. We have 32 bags to be taken into the hotel.

B : Yes, sir. Porters are here now. I'll ask them to bring in all of your bags.

A : Thank you. Can you tell me where the front desk is?

B : Go straight ahead and step down.
The front desk is right in front of you.

A : (To a guest waiting in line to check in)
Excuse me for interrupting.

E : Certainly.

A : (To a front clerk)
Who is in charge of group checking in?

C : Just a moment, sir. I'll see If he's in. There he is. Joe, your client is waiting for you at the desk.

Dialog 2

C : Good morning, sir. May I help you?

A : Good morning. I'm the tour escort of Korea Tour from Korea. My name is Kim. We have room reservations here made by Gay Travel Service's New York Office.

C : One moment, sir. Let me check our records. Here it is. It says you are a party of 32 with 15 twins and 2 singles each with bath?

A : Yes, that's our party.

C : Are there any changes in the room?

A : No, no changes so far. Are all rooms the same size? I'd like to make sure of that before I pass out room keys to our members.

C : Yes, sir. They are all the same in size.

A : Great, now give me the room keys.

C : Here they are, two keys for singles and 30 keys for 15 twin rooms. I'll have the bell captain bring your bags to your rooms.

D : I see all of your bags have yellow tags. I'll take care of them.

Useful Expressions

1. I'm the tour escort of the Korea Tour, and we've just arrived.
2. We're supposed to have reservations.
3. Welcome to our hotel.
4. A party of seventy-five.
5. We'll check out on Friday.

be supposed to + V : ~할 예정이다, ~하기로 되어있다, ~해야된다.

Unit 6 CHECKING-IN THE HOTEL (II)

▪A = Front clerk, ▪B = Tour conductor

Dialog 1

A : May I help you, sir?

B : Yes, I'm the tour escort of the Korea Survey Team, and we've just arrived. We're supposed to have reservations through Gay Tours.

A : We've been expecting you, sir. You are the party of the Korea Survey team, right?

B : Yes, we are.

A : Are you Mr. Kim?

B : No, I'm Chang. He is the chief escort.

A : Oh, excuse me, Mr. Chang. Welcome to our hotel.

B : Thank you.

Dialog 2

A : A party of seventy-three?

B : Oh, no. It's seventy-five.

A : Well, we're holding thirty-six twins and one single for seventy-three people.

B : Something's wrong. We've requested thirty seven twins and one single through Gay Tours, and it's been confirmed. You see, the voucher also says thirty-seven twins, seventy-five in total.

A : All right, sir. I'll give you another twin, which makes thirty-seven twins and one single for seventy-five, right?

B : That's right.

A : Now, I'll give you the rooming list.

B : Thank you.

Useful Expressions

1. Now it's all set, right?
2. Here are your keys.
3. One key to a room.
4. One key to each guest.
5. I'm the tour conductor.

Unit 7

RESERVATION FOR BREAKFAST

■A = Tour conductor, ■B = Head waiter, ■C = Waiter

Dialog 1

A : I'd like to talk to the head waiter about table reservations for tomorrow morning's breakfast.

C : That would be Mr. Turner. Let me check to see if he's in his office.

C : (Some time later) He's in, and he says he'll be right up here in about 5 minutes, sir. Please wait here.

B : Mr. Kim? Welcome to Hyatt Hotel, my name is Ted Turner. Glad to see you. You said something about tomorrow's breakfast?

A : Glad to see you Mr. Turner, I'd like to make a reservation for 32 people for breakfast tomorrow.

B : Be glad to have you. At what time?

A : At seven.

B : That's a bit early. Waiters do not show up here before 7:20 in the morning. We begin table serving at 7:30.

Dialog 2

A : Then, we'll have our breakfast at 7:30. Could you speed up your serving? We don't have much time in the morning.

B : Very well, then, what will you have for breakfast?

A : Show me the menu, please. Let me see, we'll have Club Breakfast No. 2. It'll be fruit juice, scrambled eggs, toast and coffee.

B : Exactly, sir. Any other arrangements?

A : Yes, I'd like to have all the table together. A pitcher of water on each table, and the tables by the windows, if possible.

B : Yes, I could do that.

A : One more thing. Please make out one check and charge it to me. I'll take care of it.

Useful Expressions

1. May I speak to the manager?
2. I'm the tour conductor.
3. We're supposed to have reservations for dinner tomorrow evening.
4. A party of fifty-five?
5. My name is Kim, Room 1508.

Unit 8 SIGHTSEEING ARRANGEMENTS

■A = Tour escort, ■B = Representative of local travel agent

Dialog 1

(Over the telephone)

A : I'd like to talk to you about our group's sightseeing program for tomorrow. Could you come to our hotel this evening?

B : Be glad to. And when and where in your hotel?

A : At six in the evening in the lobby of Hyatt Regency Hotel. Is that all right with you?

B : Certainly.

(Around 6 p.m. in the lobby of Grand Hyatt Hotel)

B : Excuse me, are you Mr. Kim of Korea Tours? I am James Jones of Pell Tours in Washington D.C.

A : That's right. Nice to meet you, Mr. Jones.

B : Glad to meet you, Mr. Kim.

A : Let's sit over there and go over the sightseeing program.

B : Yes. (showing a copy of tour itinerary to Mr. Kim) this is a full-day's excursion to Williamsburg (from Washington). You'll leave here at 8:30 in the morning and will return around 6, just before dinner time.

A : Fine. How far is it from here to Williamsburg?

B : Roughly 200 miles.

■A = Tour conductor, ■B = Tour guide

Dialog 2

A : It's a long drive. Do we stop over somewhere on the way to Williamsburg?

B : Yes, you'll have a rest stop at Fredrickburg some 50 miles from here. Then, continue for another 80 miles to Richmond. At Richmond you'll visit the Phillip Morris Cigarette Plant. I'm sure it'll be an interesting experience for your group, even for non-smokers.

A : How long do we stay in the plant?

B : About an hour or so.

A : Sounds interesting. What about lunch? Do we eat lunch in Richmond?

B : Yes, just after the plant visit. We recommend the "Miller Restaurant." It's a clean and inexpensive seafood restaurant. It's only a few minutes ride from the plant.

A : Your voucher says, "no lunch is included" in your arrangements. In other words, we'll have to pay the "Miller" direct, won't we?

B : Yes, that's right.

Dialog 3

A : Do we have to reserve tables at the "Miller?"

B : I don't think so. Since you have only 12 members, we have arranged for you to start eating at 1:30 p.m. so the restaurant service will not be rushed. It's off the peak lunch hour.

A : Fine. What can we see in Williamsburg?

B : Well, as shown in the itinerary you'll see the Governor's Palace. the Colonial Capital, the Public Gaol, Craft Shops and the National Wax Museum.

A : The admission fees for those places are not included in your tour fare, are they?

B : No, they're not. You settle your account with these establishments yourself.

A : Very well. Can you have our bus park at the hotel at 8:20 tomorrow morning?

A : Very well. Can you have our bus park at the hotel at 8:20 tomorrow morning?

B : Yes, we can.

Useful Expressions

1. I'm sorry he is not in now. Shall I have him call you back?
2. Hello, this is Kim speaking.
3. Now 1 m going to give you the schedule.
4. I'd like to see the person in charge of banquet service.
5. I'm sorry to have kept you waiting.

person in charge of banquet service : 연회 담당 책임자를 말한다.

Unit 9

SIGHTSEEING

■A = Tour escort, ■B = Guide

Dialog 1

(At Grand Hyatt Hotel on the morning of the sightseeing day)

B : I'm the driver and guide. I work for Bell Tours. My name is Sam Lima. Glad to meet you.

A : Nice meeting you, Mr. Lima. My name is Kim, the tour escort of this Korean group. Where can I see our bus?

B : It's in the garage of this hotel.

A : Good. Mr. Lima, we'll leave here at 8:30.

B : Right. We have ten more minutes to go. Do your members speak English?

A : No, not all of them. There is a language barrier. They may get what you say when you speak slowly. I'll tell them in Korean what you have said.

B : Good. We'll have an afternoon sightseeing tour in Williamsburg. In the morning I'll tell you all about the colonial days in this country on the way to Williamsburg. It's about four hours ride from here.

• **language barrier** : 언어의 장벽(의사소통이 안되는).

A : That'll be an interesting lecture tour for us. Wen you are talking about historical items, don't try to cover too much. Please pause for a few minutes in between so I can easily translate into Korean. Can you do that?

B : Yes, I can.

A : Can you jot down for me the years when you talk about the important historical events?

B : Sure, I can.

A : Everyone's here now. We can start now.

Dialog 2

B : We are now southern end of Williamsburg. We'll visit the Information Center to see an outline map of Williamsburg.

A : What else can we study at the Information Center?

B : You can obtain an Official Guidebook. You can also see a free orientation film in Korean?

A : In Korean?

B : Yes, the orientation is taped in six languages including Korean.

A : Now, we'll get off the bus to see the Center.

B : Bus will be locked, but please don't leave any of your belongings in the bus.

A : No, we won't.

(In the Information Center)

B : Here is an outline map of Williamsburg. We are here now in the Center. I'll mark the places where our bus stops. First, we go anticlockwise on Nicolson Street to the Public Gaol.

A : What's the Public Gaol?

B : It's a sort of jail. In 1718, Blackbeard's Pirates were captured and imprisoned here before being hanged. In Colonial days, debtors and criminals were confined here.

Dialog 3

A : What will we see next?

B : The Capitol. The Capitol is located within walking distance from the Gaol. You will walk down there. No vehicles are allowed to park around there. In ten minutes I'll have the bus turned out there.

A : I got it. When will we visit the Governor's Palace?

B : We'll see the Palace at the end of the tour in Williamsburg. The places we'll see next are the Magazine and National Wax Museum. There again, in twenty minutes the bus will be there to pick you up.

A : Very well.

B : Our tour in Williamsburg will end at the Governor's Palace, which once served as a residence of the royal governors. There are extensive formal gardens and dependencies.

Dialog 4

A : Do we have time for a brief sightseeing of the craftshops?

B : Yes, the bus will pass by the streets that are lined with a variety of craftshops including that of a cabinetmaker, wigmaker, blacksmith, silversmith, gunsmith, harnessmaker, baker, basketmaker, cooper, galt apothecary, jeweler and clockmaker, printer and bookbinder. I think that'll be all for this town.

A : What's apothecary?

B : It's the colonial drugstore.

A : I see. Now, how much time did you say will be spent in this Center? About one hour, right?

B : I think it's enough including the time for watching the orientation film. Now, you can see the cafeteria over there. Rest rooms are on the left side of the lobby. Then, I'll see you at 2:30 right here.

A : Very well, see you later.

Useful Expressions

1. She is a guide from the travel agency.
2. Have you ever been here before?
3. Then you're familiar with the course, aren't you?
4. Shall we dissuss the schedule?
5. The buses will be here at 8:30 and we'll leave at 9:00.
6. First we go to the Opera House, then Golden Gate Park.

Unit 10

SHOPPING

■A = Korean traveler, ■B = Store clerk

Dialog 1

A : Where can I buy books?

B : Hardbacks or paperbacks?

A : Both.

B : Books are sold on the fifth floor and paperbacks on the street level.

A : Can you tell me where the escalator is?

B : Up escalators?

A : Yes.

B : Go straight ahead and turn to the left at the end of the corridor.

A : ... I'll take these books.

B : Seven dollars per copy, please.

A : Do you accept traveler's checks?

B : Yes, we do. Can I see your ID card?

A : Yes, here it is (showing the clerk the passport). Can you gift wrap it?

B : The gift wrapping counter is in the lower floor.

A : Thank you.

ID card(=Identification card) : 신분증.(우리나라에선 주민등록증이 이에 해당한다).
ID Card No. : 주민등록번호(Identification card number)

Dialog 2

A : Do you have fountain pens?

B : Yes, we do. I'll show you some.

A : Let me try to write with this one. It writes well. How much is it for half a dozen?

B : Three dollars per pen, 18 dollars altogether.

A : Can you discount a bit?

B : Sorry, we can't give you any discount.

A : Can I try on this jacket?

B : Certainly, the fitting booth is right over there.

A : I think the shoulder looks a bit baggy.

B : Does it? The light's not too good here.

A : I like these patch-pockets, but the jacket seems to me a little too flashy. Can you show me some sober ones?

B : Sorry, we don't have any subdued color jacket in stock.

A : Then let's forget about jackets. Do you have any wash-n-dry pants?

B : Yes, we have. I'll show you some.

A : Show me some cuffless pants. My waist measures 25 inches.

B : Very well.

try on : (의류, 신발 등을) 입어 (신어, 써) 보다.
Can I try on this hat?
Yes, you can. You can try it on.

A: I'll take this one. How much do I owe you?

B: It's 8 dollars. Please pay the cashier over there, thank you.

A: Thank you.

Useful Expressions

1. Where can I buy books?
2. Do you accept traveler's checks?
3. I'm just looking.
4. I'll take this one.
5. Show me how to use it. Would you show me how to handle chopsticks?

Unit 11

PLANT VISIT

▪A = Tour escort, ▪B = Mr. Moran, ▪C = Operator

Dialog 1

(Telephone conversation)

A : Hello, is Mr. Moran in? I mean, Mr. Oliver Moran, the plant manager.

C : Yes, he is. May I ask your name, please?

A : I am Mr. Kim, and I'd like to talk to him about the pre-arranged plant visit.

C : Hold on, Mr. Kim.

B : Mr. Moran speaking.

A : Mr. Moran? This is Mr. Kim. I'd like to double check with you some items about the plant visit for tomorrow.

B : Yes, I have a letter from Evandale Chamber of Commerce that you are coming here tomorrow morning.

A : Could you tell me how to reach your plant? I'm now in the Evandale Motor Inn.

B : Oh, are you? Then, drive along the Nelson Highway until you come to Evandale Point. The landmark will be an old brick building with a Chevy Ad on its roof located at the junction of Nelson Highway and Evandale Point.

A : Yes.

B : There turn to the left and continue driving for about 20 minutes and our plant is on the right side. You can enter our plant through Gate 9. When you come to our plant, first see Mr. Gibson, Personnel Manager at the reception office. He will tell you what he can do for you.

A : Very well. Now speaking of the arrival time, I have your notice which says that we have to be there before 9 a.m. Right?

B : Yes, exactly.

Dialog 2

A : Then, we'll manage to arrive at your plant around 8:30 a.m.

B : That'll be fine, Mr. Kim. Anything else?

A : I have some problems.

B : You do? What are they?

A : All of our members are taking cameras with them since in the afternoon we'll go on a sightseeing tour in the town. Your notice says no camera is allowed.

B : No problem. Just bring your cameras along. Mr. Gibson will take care of those cameras when you check in at the reception office and he'll keep them while you are on a plant visit with us.

A : That's very kind of you, Mr. Moran.

B : You're welcome.

A : Other items in your notice have already been told to our team members. they are: no tape recording, putting on walking shoes, and our group will be split into three smaller groups and will follow your assigned guides.

B : Exactly, Mr. Kim.

A : Very well, then, I'll be seeing you tomorrow morning, Mr. Moran.

B : Fine, thank you for calling, Mr. Kim.

Useful Expressions

1. May I speak to Mr. Hopkins of Public Relations?
2. I'll connect you to Public Relations.
3. We're a party from Korea.
4. I want to talk about our visit to your firm tomorrow.
5. Which hotel are you staying at?

Unit 12

APPOINTMENT BY TELEPHONE

■A = Tour escort, ■B = Mr. Smith(Travel agent)

Dialog 1

(On the telephone)

A : Hello, Mr. Smith, this is Mr. Oh, the tour escort of Korean group traveling in the U.S.A.

B : Well, Mr. Oh, what's on your mind?

A : I hope you remember me. I was at the PATA Conference in Seoul last winter. At that time, I promised you I'd provide you with some information about the destinations frequently visited by Korean travelers.

B : Mr. Oh, I remember now.

A : Yes, I've brought a report with me. In it, there are more than a dozen destinations in the U.S.A. with total numbers of Korean visited these sites.

B : Really, it's very kind of you, Mr. Oh.

provide A with B : A에게 B를 공급하다(대어준다).

Dialog 2

A : I am planning to give the report to you tomorrow. We are staying here for a couple of days, and I will find time tomorrow at lunch.

B : Sorry, but I have a previous appointment for tomorrow's lunch. What about after 7 tomorrow evening?

A : I can find time after 7:30. Dinner would be excellent. Is it too late for you?

B : No, 7:30 is quite all right. Shall we meet at 7:30 at the Breelands? Their seafoods are excellent.

A : Very well, Mr. Smith, then, I'll be at the Breelands at 7:30 tomorrow evening. I'll tell you all about the movement of Korean travelers tomorrow.

B : I hope so, see you tomorrow evening. Thank you for calling me. Mr. Oh.

Useful Expressions

1. I hope you remember me.
2. We met at the Korea House in Seoul.
3. What about after seven tomorrow evening?
4. I want to see you.
5. Thank you for calling me.

Unit 13 FOOD SERVICE

▪A = Tour escort, ▪B = Restaurant employee

Dialog 1

(Making reservations by phone)

A : Hello, Skylon Tower Restaurant? I have a group of 12 people. We'd like to have dinner at your restaurant around 7:30 this evening. Can you reserve for us good tables near the window commanding a fine view?

B : Twelve people around 7:30? We're a bit busy that time. Could you make it at 8?

A : All right, we can. We'll be there at 8. This is Mr. Han, tour escort of Korean team. Can you have all the tables put together?

B : Yes, we can. Thank you for calling. See you later, sir.

(At the restaurant)

B : Good evening Mr. Han. Are all of your people here?

A : Yes, we're all here.

B : Good. May I take your order, sir? Here is a wine list. Would you care for some cocktail?

A : Yes, three red Burgundies, two sherries, and 7 beers, please.

B : What brand of beer?

A : What brand do you have?

B : We have Ham, Miller, Schlitz and Bud.

A : Give us Ham, please.

B：Any appetizers that go with the cocktails?

A：Shrimp cocktails for all of us, please.

B：Very well, and soup?

A：Eleven onion soups, please.

B：Entrees?

A：Give us a little time to decide.

B：Take your time, sir. (Some time later)

B：Have you decided, sir?

A：Yes, eleven roast beefs and one roast leg of lamb, please.

B：Vegetables?

A：No vegetables.

B：And to follow?

A：We'll decide later.

B：Very well, sir.

A: And for salad twelve hearts of lettuce, please.

B：Very well, sir. Now may I take your order for dessert?

A：Yes, ten strawberry shortcakes.

B：Beverages?

A：Ten coffees and one milk, please

B：Yes, sir, thank you very much.

A：And our people drink lots of water. Can we have pitchers of water on each table?

B：Yes, we'll bring pitchers right away.

Dialog 2

A：Excellent food, delicious.

B：Thank you, sir.

A：Check, please. Make one check and bill it to me.

B : Yes, sir, here it is.

A : How much is it?

B : 340 dollars, sir.

A : Does it include tax and service charge?

B : Yes, all included.

A : Is this Diners Club credit card honored here?

B : Yes, it is (honored).

A : Here you are.

B : May I have your signature here?

A : Certainly.

B : Thank you very much, sir, please come again.

Useful Expressions

1. I suppose the reservation has been made by Gay Tours.
2. This is the table d'hôte and this is á la carte.
3. Hot consomme, please.
4. Green salad with French dressing, please.
5. Strawberry ice cream, please.

'coffee 다섯 잔 주세요'라고 주문할 때는 "Five coffees, please"하면 된다.
'홍차 세 잔 주세요'는 "Three teas, please"
'cockail 하지 않은 whisky 두 잔 주세요'는 "Two straight whiskies, please"하면 된다. 얼음을 탈 땐 'whisky on the rocks.'

Unit 14 RENT-A-CAR

▪A = Korean traveler, ▪B = Rent-a-car office's staff

Dialog 1

B : May I help you?

A : Yes, I'd like to rent a car. What kind of cars do you have?

B : We have the latest model of Ford and other fine cars. May I see your driving licence?

A : Yes, here it is. It's an International Driving Permit.

B : Do you have any identification cards besides this license?

A : I have my passport here.

B : Great, that's the surest thing.

A : Can you tell me the rental charge?

B : The national average daily rate is $50 for 24 hours.

A : What items are included in the rental charge?

B : It includes gas, oil and insurance, regardless of how many rides.

Dialog 2

A : Can you give me any discount for a week rental?

B : Yes, that's averaging $200.

A : Is your rental system carried out on a "rent it here and leave it there" basis?

B : Yes, that's the way we do exactly.

A : Then, may I rent your new Ford for two days?

B : Sure, go easy with your driving and be aware of our traffic that keeps to the right. Here is your key for the car. Have a pleasant driving.

A : Thank you, I will.

Dialog 3

A : Could you arrange a rental car for us?

B : Yes, of course, we can. But only for those participating in the convention.

A : Oh, great. What's the charge?

B : Well, the basic charge for a '88 Pontiac or Ford is twenty five dollars a day and thirty cents per running mile. Tax and insurance are not included.

A : I'd like to rent two Fords for ten o'clock in the morning the day after tomorrow.

B : All right. Will you fill in this form, please? And you'll have to pay a deposit of thirty dollars per car. Will you be using a credit card or paying cash?

A : I'll pay cash. You'll deliver the cars here, won't you?

B : Yes. The cars will be here at the O'Farrell Street entrance the day after tomorrow morning, so pick up your keys at this desk at nine fifty.

A : Where do I turn in the keys?

B : Just turn in the keys here and pay the balance if it's before six in the evening.

Useful Expressions

1. I'd like to rent a car.
2. Do you have any I.D. card?
3. Here is your key.
4. What's the charge?
5. I'll pay cash.

Unit 15

CHECKING-OUT

▪A = Tour conductor, ▪B = Cashier, ▪C = Bell captain

Dialog 1

A : I'm the tour conductor of the Korea Survey Team, and we'll checking out tomorrow morning. Would you please have our bills ready by then?

B : Yes, sir. The Korea Survey Team? Your name and room number, please?

A : My name is Kim, fifteen-oh-eight.

B : All right, sir. What time are you leaving?

A : We're leaving at ten o'clock. What time do you want me to come down here to settle the account?

B : Oh, let's see. How about nine? I'll have everything ready for you by then.

Dialog 2

B : Are you going to have breakfast?

A : Yes, we'll have it in the banquet room.

B : Do you want the charge billed to your master account?

A : Yes, please do so.

B : Do you want the porterage charged to the account, too?

A : Well, no, I'll pay it in cash to the bell captain.

B : Very well. Does everybody pay for his incidental charge?

A : No, I'll pay them all. By the way, we've already remitted a down payment of two thousand dollars to you through the bank. I want you to check it. This is a copy of remittance.

B : Just a moment, please. I'll see if it's already in.

A : Thank you.

B : Yes, we've received your remittance. We'll deduct this amount from the total charges when you pay them tomorrow morning.

A : Fine. See you at nine o'clock tomorrow morning.

B : Thank you very much.

Dialog 3

A : I'm the tour conductor of the group leaving here at ten o'clock tomorrow morning, and I'd like to know what time will you start bringing down the luggage?

B : Yes, sir. Which group is yours?

A : The Korea Survey Team.

B : Okay, sir. How many pieces of luggage do you have?

A : Seventy-seven. Seventy-five suitcases and two carton boxes.

B : Okay. What time are you leaving?

A : We're leaving at ten, but the coaches will be hired by nine forty-five.

B : There're two other groups checking out at the same time. I'd appreciate if you'd let us start at eight.

A : Eight o'clock? I guess it's all right. Do you want us to put our luggage outside the room?

B : No. Just leave them in the room. Our men will take care of them.

A : Fine. Tell them to just collect the suitcases only. Our people will bring the other small bags themselves.

B : All right. Your name and room number, please.

A : My name is Kim, fifteen-oh-eight.

B : We'll take care of it, Mr. Kim.

A : Thank you.

Useful Expressions

1. I'm checking out tomorrow morning.
2. Are you going to have breakfast?
3. See you tomorrow.
4. I hope you enjoyed your stay.
5. We're leaving at 11:30.

Unit 16 CHECKING-IN(AT THE AIRPORT)

■A = Representative from local travel agent, ■B = Tour conductor, ■C = Ground agent

Dialog 1

A : Are they all on board?

B : Yes. Everybody's on. Shall we go now?

A : Okay. Let's go.

B : How long does it take to the airport?

A : Oh, about half an hour at this time of day. I imagine it may take a little bit till we get on the freeway.

B : 1s that so? We have plenty of time even then, haven't we?

A : Oh, yes. Your flight's leaving at ten, right?

B : Yes, you're right. American Airlines.

A : What is the flight number?

B : One eighty-two.

A : All right.

Dialog 2

B : Good morning. A group to Chicago, please.

C : Good morning. Your tickets, please.

B : Here they are.

C : How many passengers?

B : Seventy-five.

C : Are you taking Flight one eighty-two for Chicago?
B : That's right.
C : Okay. How many pieces of luggage do you have?
B : We have seventy-seven. They're being unloaded from the coaches now.
C : All right. I'll have the skycaps handle them.
B : Thank you. I told the skycaps once when we arrived here.
C : I see. I'll make sure of them. One moment, please.

Useful Expressions

1. You'll have your boarding pass at the gate.
2. I'm going to take your flight 240 for Seoul.
3. May we have it on the scale, please?
4. Which seat would you prefer, sir?
5. I think I will take a window seat.
6. I'm here to check in.

aisle seat : 통로측 좌석.
window seat : 창측 좌석.(밖의 경관을 볼 수 있어 좋다)
no smoking section : 금연석.

Unit 17 USEFUL EXPRESSIONS

1. Do you have anything to declare? /No, I have nothing to declare. (= No, I don't have anything to declare.)
2. These are my personal belongings.
3. This is an instant-food. I'll eat it myself.
4. This is a gift for my friend.
5. May I see the menu?
6. Can you take away this dish?
7. Give me some water.
8. Fry the eggs sunny-side up.
9. I'll have my coffee with no sugar and no cream.
10. Can I have some more coffee?
11. May I have a fork?
12. This is not the dish I ordered.
13. I don't eat fish.
14. Is this an express elevator?
15. Is the coffee shop still open?
16. Where is the rest room?

화장실에 대한 용어 : rest room : 극장 등에 있는, bath room : 가정이나 호텔에 있는, men's room 또는 gen's room : 남성 전용의, ladies' room : 여성전용의 화장실을 물을 때, Where can I wash my hands?라는 간접적인 표현도 쓰인다.

17. Do I have to line up here?

18. What happened in the lobby?

19. Any messages for me?

20. I'll stay here until September 20th.

21. Keep this bag for two hours.

22. Is it raining outside? (Is it snowing outside?)

23. I'll hang up the phone.

24. Wake me up at six tomorrow morning.

25. Make my bed.

26. When can I have the laundry returned?

27. One whisky on the rocks, please.

28. May I have an extra blanket?

29. Come in.

30. Don't disturb.

31. I'll fly to Seoul.

32. I'll fly Korea Air Lines.

33. This is one of my baggage.

34. My baggage has a yellow tag.

35. I don't have much time. I have lots of time.

36. Hurry up?

37. I must go back to the hotel by 5 p.m.

38. I'll come up there.

39. What time is it now?
40. May I ask your name?
41. Go ahead.
42. Wait a minute.
43. How do you do?
44. How do you do? Pleased to meet you.
45. Will you do me a favor?
46. I'm sorry to have bothered you.
47. You're welcome.
48. Can I swim here?
49. Can I use the ticket?
50. Can I enter the church?
51. Is there any post office near here?
52. I want to go this place.
53. How far is it from here to the airport?
54. How long does it take from here to the subway station?
55. How much does it cost from here to the station by taxi?
56. Tell me the way to the railroad station.
57. Is this the right way to the theater?
58. How much is the entrance fee?

시간을 물을 때 : 'What time do you have?' 또는 'You've got the time, haven't you?'라는 표현이 부드럽다. 이름을 물을 때도, 'Can I have your name?'이라는 표현이 부드럽다.

59. Is the museum closed today?

60. May I take your picture?

61. Is it all right to take a picture of the building?

62. Where can I buy fountain pens?

63. I'm just looking. Can I have a look?

64. How much is it?

65. That's too high.

66. Show me smaller ones.

67. I'll take them.

68. Can you give me any discount?

69. I don't need.

70. Can I pay in Korean won?

71. Do you accept traveler's checks?

72. Wrap it up.

73. Can you deliver it to my hotel?

74. May I try it on?

75. Do I have to go to the cashier?

76. What is it made of?

77. Hold it for a moment.

78. Give me the change.

79. Give me a receipt.

80. Break this into coins.

81. How late do you open?

82. She is ill in bed.

83. I have a headache.

84. Will you call a doctor for me?

85. My money was stolen.

86. I have lost my passport.

87. My watch is out of order.

88. My money was robbed.

89. My suitcase is broken.

90. My room is too noisy.

91. The towel is not clean.

92. The light bulb burnt out.

93. I left my key in the room and the door was locked.

94. I spilt milk on the floor.

95. How can I turn off the light?

96. I can't find my suitcase.

97. I can't open the door with the key.

98. I spent all of my money.

99. I missed the bus.

100. I forgot to bring it here.

break into coins : 주전으로 바꿔달라는 표현으로.
Would you break this 10,000 won note? : 이 10,000원 권 지폐를 잔돈으로 바꿔 주십시오? 라는 표현.
Would you break this 1,000 won note into coins?(이 1,000원짜리 지폐를 주전으로 바꿔 주세요.)
- party나 식사 등이 진행 중일 때 화장실에 잠깐 다녀올 때는, "I'll be back soon."이란 멋스러운 표현이 있다.

PART V

SITUATIONAL DIALOGS

Unit 1 INTRODUCTION

■A = Mr. Smith, ■B = Mr. Brown, ■C = Mr. Kim

Dialog

A : Mr. Brown, may I introduce Mr. Kim?
B : I'm glad to meet you.
C : How do you do, Mr. Brown?
B : Mr. Smith tells me you're from Korea?
C : That's right. I work for an electric company.
B : What's your position there?
C : I'm just an engineer.
A : Just an engineer? Mr. Kim has designed a unique transistor radio. He's not "just an engineer!"
B : Korean people are very humble.
C : May I ask what you do, Mr. Brown?
B : Sure. I'm a computer systems analyst.

Useful Expressions

1. Mr. Brown, I'd like to introduce Mr. Kim.
2. We have a guest with us today. He's Mr. Kim from Seoul.
3. How do you do? This is my first trip to Chicago.
4. My name is Sangho Kim. Please call me Sangho.
5. What do you do for a living? I teach in Korea.

상대방의 직업을 물을 때에 **What's your job?** 또는 **What's your occupation?**이란 표현을 쓸 수 있으나 너무 딱딱하고 formal하기 때문에 일상회화에서는 **"What do you do for a living?"**이란 표현이 부드럽고 좋다.

Unit 2

AIRLINE TRAVEL ARRANGEMENTS

▪A = Clerk, ▪B = Mr. Kim

Dialog

A : Hello, good morning. May I help you, sir?

B : Yes. Good morning. I'd like an air ticket.

A : Where to? Where would you like to fly to?

B : I would like to go to Los Angeles. Er, economy class, please. Not first class; it's too expensive.

A : All right. Single or return?

B : Return. I'm going on holidays. Do you have any cheaper tickets?

A : Yes. Night flights, excursion tickets.... Er, when's the ticket for?

B : The day after tomorrow.

Unit 3 CHECK-IN(AT THE AIRPORT)

■A = Mr. Park, ■B = Clerk

Dialog

A : Is this the Pan American Airways check-in?

B : Yes, it is. Your ticket, please.

A : Wait a minute. I seem to have lost it. Oh, here it is.

B : (Checking the ticket) Return to New York. Flight 800.

A : Which gate do I go to?

B : It'll be announced.

Announcer : Pan American Airways announces the departure of Flight 800 bound for New York via Fairbanks. Will passengers for this flight please go to Gate 6?

B : Gate 6, sir. Luggage?

A : Just this case.

B : (Putting the case on the weighing machine) Nineteen kilograms. That's all right. You don't have any hand luggage?

A : No.

B : Your boarding pass.

A : Thank you.

Unit 4 BEFORE TAKE-OFF

■A = Mrs. Kim, ■B = Stewardess

Dialog

Announcer : On behalf of Air France, Captain Steve and his crew would like to welcome you on board this aircraft.

Our flying time to San Francisco will be six hours, and we shall be flying at a height of 6,000 meters. We hope you will enjoy your flight.

A : Can I have something to drink?

B : Yes, but after take-off, ma'am. Can you wait till after take-off? We'll take off soon. Please fasten your seat belt.

A : Certainly. Please show me how to use this seat belt.

B : Yes, ma'am. Just like this. Is this tight enough?

A : Yes, that's fine.

taking off : 이륙.
landing : 착륙.
fasten seat belt : 안전벨트를 매다.

Unit 5 BEVERAGE SREVICE(ON THE PLANE)

■A = Stewardess, ■B = Mr. Lee

Dialog

A : Would you care for a drink?

B : Yes, please. May I have a dry martini?

B : (getting the service) Thank you. How rich is it?

A : One dollar, sir.

B : I'm sorry but I don't have any small American money with me. May I pay in traveller's check?

A : Certainly, sir.

care for=like : 좋아하다. Would you care for a cup of coffee? No. I don't care for coffee. 주의할 일은 'care for'란 표현은 의문문, 부정문에만 사용하도록 권합니다.

Unit 6 FOOD SERVICE(ON THE PLANE)

■A = Stewardess, ■B = Mrs. Kim

Dialog

A : Please return your seat to the upright position. It's about time for your dinner.

B : Thank you.

A : Which would you prefer, lobster or steak?

B : Lobster, please. And may I have another beer?

A : Certainly, ma'am. Would you like some dressing?

B : Let me see... I'd like to have some of this kind. And may I have some more bread and butter?

A : Certainly, ma'am. Just a minute, please.

Unit 7

CHANGING FLIGHTS

■A = Ground hostess, ■B = Mr. Park

A : Are you a transit passenger, sir?

B : No, I'm changing flights. I'm going to Dallas on Northwest Orient Airlines Flight 10.

A : Please wait in the airport lobby.

B : What should I do with my checked baggage?

A : It'll be automatically transferred to your nex flight.

B : I think I have some two hours before my connecting flight leaves for Dallas. Can I go out and look around the city?

A : Do as you please.

Unit 8 THE DISEMBARKATION CARD

■A = Mr. Park, ■B = Stewardess

Announcement : Ladies and gentlemen. We'll arrive in Singapore in half an hour. The local time is 6:40 p.m. The weather's fair, and the temperature is 83 degrees Fahrenheit. Thank you.

A : It was a nice flight.

B : Are you getting off at Singapore?

A : Yes, I am.

B : Please fill in the disembarkation card and the baggage declaration form.

A : I've completed the disembarkation card. Will you please check it for me?

B : Let me take a look at it. It's almost complete. Now, you just have to write your visa number and the date of issue here.

disembarkation card : 입국신고서(흔히 landing card 라고 함).
baggage declaration card : 세관 신고서.

Announcements on various occasions

• Welcome announcement

Ladies and gentlemen. Welcome aboard Air India. Please make certain once more that your seat belt is fastened, and observe the no smoking sign until it is turned off. We hope you'll enjoy your flight.

• Life preserver demonstration

Ladies and gentlemen. It is not likely that you'll have to use a life preserver or an oxygen mask during this flight. However, in case they should become necessary, we'd like to demonstrate how to use them.

• Arrival announcement

Ladies and gentlemen. We have just landed at Honolulu International Airport. The local time here in Honolulu is 10:30. Please remain seated until this aircraft comes to a complete halt. All passengers are requested to have their passports, vaccination certificates and disembarkation cards ready for inspection by the authorities in charge.

no smoking sign : 비행기 이 · 착륙시 흡연금지 신호(램프 글자에 불이 들어온다.) fasten seat belt sign도 불이 들어온다.

Signs in the Aircraft

Fasten Seat Belt:

No Smoking:

Exit:

Toilets/Lavatory:

Sanitary Napkins:

Hand Towels Only:

Vacant:

Occupied:

Bag Disposal:

Ash Tray:

Airsick Bags:

Push Button:

Flush Toilet:

Used Blades:

Call Button:

Coat Hook:

Signs in Toilets

Please Lock Door:

No Smoking in Toilets:

No Cigarette Disposal:

Unit 9

IMMIGRATION

■A = Officer, ■B = Miss Kang

A : Vaccination certificate, please.

B : Here it is.

A : Passport, please. And show me your landing card, too.

B : Here they are.

A : How long are you going to stay here in Chicago?

B : About two weeks.

A : What's the purpose of your visit here?

B : I'm going to attend the 15th International Computer Convention.

A : Are you? Now, please go to Customs.

B : Where is it?

A : That way. Follow the arrows.

Unit 10

CUSTOMS

▪A = Officer, ▪B = Mr. Park

A : Show me your passport and customs declaration form, please.

B : Certainly. Here you are.

A : Do you have anything to declare?

B : I don't think so. Only my personal effects.

A : May I see your trunks?

B : Must I open them?

A : Yes, it's the rule. What's in this package?

B : It's a Korean-made doll. A present for a friend of mine in San Francisco.

A : Do you have any other gifts?

B : Yes. I have three Korean amethyst rings, a pearl necklace and a set of chinaware here in this box.

Unit 11

TAXI-CAB

▪A = Mr. Kang, ▪B = Cab driver

A : (to the cab driver) Hello, can you recommend me a good hotel in this town?

B : Certainly. I'd recommend you YMCA hotel. That's not far from here.

A : Sounds good. Is the price there reasonable?

B : I think so.

A : Double your tip for a cigarette, please.

B : I'm sorry, sir. I don't smoke. Now, here we are.

A : How much do I owe you?

B : Five dollars, sir.

Unit 12 HOTEL RESERVATION

▪A = Miss Han, ▪B = Clerk

A : Hello. I'd like to make a reservation, please.

B : Very well. When and how long would you like to stay here?

A : On Saturday and Sunday nights.

B : What kind of room would you like to have?

A : A single room with bath, please.

B : All right. May I have your name, please?

A : My name is Miss Sun-Hae Han.

B : The charge is 295 dollars per night, plus tax and service charge.

A : That's all right. I'll check in at 4 o'clock this afternoon.

Unit 13 HOTEL REGISTRATION

■A = Clerk, ■B = Mr. Kim

A : Would you fill in this registration form, please.

B : Certainly. Here you are.

A : Thank you, sir. Here's your key, sir. Room 2152. The bellboy will take your bags and show you to your room.

B : Which floor is it on?

A : It's on the 21st floor. It's an outside room, facing the river.

B : Wonderful. Does the room have a private bath?

A : Yes. Plus ice-making machine and a very nice view of the river.

B : And what's the price of a room?

A : It's 275 dollars a day, excluding the tax and the service charge.

Unit 14 OVERSEAS PHONE CALL

▪A = Mr. Han, ▪B = Operator, ▪C = Overseas operator

A : I'd like to make an overseas call to my wife.

B : Yes. Where to, sir?

A : To Seoul, Korea.

B : Hold on, please. I'll call the overseas operator for you. (a little later)

C : Hello. This is the overseas operator. What number do you wish to call?

A : I'd like to make a collect call to Mrs. Han In-Ja in Seoul, Korea. Her number is 566-2935.

C : I see.

A : How much time will it take to get through to Seoul?

C : About 30 minutes, sir.

A : Thank you. And what's the toll?

C : It'll be 20 dollars for the first three minutes and an extra 3 dollars for every additional minute, sir.

collect call : (국제전화 등에서) 수신인 요금 부담의 전화
make a collect call.
make an overseas call. 국제전화를 하다.

Unit 15 GOING TO A RESTAURANT

■A = Mr. Martin, ■B = Mr. Chang

A : What kind of food do you like, Mr. Kim?

B : I like all kinds of food.

A : Oh really? Where would you like to go?

B : I don't know any places around here.

A : I know a great Thai restaurant. It's only three blocks from here.

B : Oh. Well, I guess we could go there.

A : You don't sound very excited about it.

B : To tell you the truth, I think Thai food is too hot.

A : How about a steakhouse?

B : That sounds better.

(in the restaurant)

A : What would you like to drink?

B : I'd like a bottle of beer.

A : How about something to go with the drink?

B : I'll have some peanuts.

A : OK. Now please order anything you like.

B : Thank you very much.

A : Why don't you get a big steak? I hear beef is very expensive in Korea.

B : It is, and I will!

A : Well, I'll order for both of us. How would you like your steak?

B : Medium, please.

미국 가정에서의 식사초대는 아주 친밀한 사이라야 베푸는 최고의 환영인데, 간단한 선물이라도 가지고 가는 것이 예의일 것이며 식사 전에 "음료 좀 드시겠습니까?"는 "Would you care for some thing to drink before dinner?"라고 합니다. 식사 때는 가벼운 이야기로 즐겁게 무드를 조성할 것이며, 심각한 업무상의 일은 피하는 것이 좋겠다. 특히 우리 동양인이 조심할 것은 식사 중, 소리를 내는 일 따위가 없도록 할 것.

Unit 16 PUBLIC TRANSPORTATION

■A = Mr. Kim, ■B = Ticket Agent, ■C = Man in the street

A : Give me a one-way ticket to New York.

B : Here you are. That will be twenty-two dollars and a half.

A : Where do I have to change trains?

B : You don't have to, unless you take the local.

A : What time does the next express leave?

B : At 9:30. You have plenty of time to catch it.

A : Which platform does the train leave from?

B : From No. 12.

A : Thanks for all your help.

B : Don't mention it. It's a part of my job.

(In New York)

A : Excuse me. Where can I get a taxi?

C : At the bus terminal. It's three blocks over there.

A : Thanks a lot. Why aren't there any taxis at this train station?

C : I don't know.

one way ticket↔round ticket.

Unit 17

INVITATIONS

■A = Mr. Kim, ■B = Tom

A : Tom, I'd like to invite you to have dinner with us.

B : Thank you very much. I always look forward to your wife's great Korean cooking.

A : It's nice of you to say so.

B : When will it be?

A : Next Saturday. We're inviting the Clarks, the Lunds and Jill Walker.

B : Sounds like a party? Not just dinner.

A : Well, you can call it whatever you like. Just be sure to come.

B : I wouldn't miss it for the world. I'm playing golf that afternoon until 6:00. What time should I get there?

A : The party is going to start at seven. Why don't you come over a little after that?

B : That would be fine.

A : And don't eat anything before you come.

B : I'll starve myself all day. You don't have to worry about me not eating enough.

A : Okay. See you Saturday.

B : Thanks again. I'm looking forward to it.

Unit 18 ASKING DIRECTIONS

■A = Mr. Kwon, ■B = Dweller

A : Excuse me.

B : Yes, can I help you?

A : Where can I find a drugstore around here?

B : Turn left at the corner. There's one a few stores down on your side of the street.

A : On my side of the street?

B : Yes. I mean on this side. You can't miss it.

A : Thank you very much. Is it Walgreen Drugstore?

B : I'm not sure. It's either Walgreen or Rexall. Is it important?

A : Well, yes it is.

B : Why? What kind of medicine are you going to buy?

A : Oh, I'm not going to buy any medicine.

B : Then why are you going to the drugstore?

A : I'm hungry. I want to eat at the lunch counter.

B : Well, what difference does it make whether it's a Walgreen drugstore, Rexall drugstore, or any other kind of drugstore?

A : Well, I love the strawberry shortcake at Walgreen's.

B : I hope you find what you're looking for.

A : Thank you for all the help.

Unit 19 AT THE BANK

■A = Bank Clerk. ■B = Mr. Choi

A : May I help you?

B : Yes, please. I'd like to open a checking account.

A : Fine. Will you fill out this form, please?

B : Certainly.

A : How much are you going to put in your account today?

B : I'll take $500 out of my savings account and put it in the checking account.

A : All right. Will this be a joint checking account?

B : I'm sorry. I don't understand what you mean.

A : Are you married?

B : Yes, I am. Why do you ask?

A : Well, do you want your wife to be able to write checks, too?

B : I don't know. I haven't thought about that.

A : Most couples today have joint checking accounts.

B : Well, okay. You can put my wife's name down, too.

A : Certainly.

B : How much do you charge per check?

A : Nothing if you keep a minimum balance of $200 in your account.

B : I hope we can do that.

Unit 20 AT THE POST OFFICE

■A = Postal Clerk, ■B = Mr. Cho

A : Can I help you?

B : Yes. I'd like to send this by airmail.

A : Where is it going?

B : To Korea.

A : Seoul?

B : No, Incheon.

A : Well, I guess the rate's the same. What does it contain?

B : It contains magazines.

A : Then you can get the special rate by sending it as printed matter.

B : Oh, is that cheaper?

A : Yes, it is. Quite a bit. You aren't sending it to a school or a library, are you?

B : No. Would that make a difference?

A : Well, sometimes there's a special rate for educational materials.

B : Well, I'm just sending this to a friend. Actually it contains men's magazines.

A : I see. But you could really call them educational materials, couldn't you?

B : Maybe. But my friend always brags that he knows everything about women already. So I suppose I'm not "educating" him.

Unit 21 AT THE PHARMACY

■A = Mr. Kwon, ■B = Druggist

A : Do you have any medicine for an upset stomach?

B : Yes. We have several kinds.

A : Well, I have a stomachache and I need some medicine.

B : How long have you had the pain?

A : Since yesterday afternoon. I thought it was something that would just go away.

B : Have you had this kind of trouble before?

A : Yes. But not very often.

B : Have you been to the doctor?

A : No, it's not that serious. Now do you have any medicine for me?

B : Yes, this one will be good.

A : How much is it?

B : It's three dollars and forty-two cents, including the tax.

A : Okay. Here's a five.

B : There you are. Here's your change. I hope you feel better soon.

A : Thank you. I'm sure I will.

Unit 22

PHONE CALL

■A = Operator, ■B = Mr. Chang, ■C = Mr. Baker

A : Baxter's Audio Supplies. May I help you?

B : Hello. Is Mr. Thompson in?

A : I'm sorry, but he is out right now. May I take a message?

B : Well, then I'd like to speak to Mr. White.

A : Mr. White isn't in this department. Do you know this extension?

B : I'm afraid not.

A : I'll look it up for you then. May I ask who's calling?

B : Yes. My name's Mr. Oh. I'm with an electric company.

A : Will you hold the line, please?

B : Certainly.

C : Hello, Mr. Oh? Sorry to keep you waiting.

B : Oh, hello, Mr. White. Don't worry about it.

C : What can I do for you this morning?

B : Do you have any free time this afternoon or tomorrow?

C : Well it's a pretty busy time of the year for us. I may be able to spare a few minutes tomorrow afternoon. Do you think you could make it between 2:45 and 3:30?

B : I'm sure I could.

C : Fine. See you tomorrow. Thank you for calling.

B : You're welcome. See you tomorrow around 2:45.

PART VI

GUIDE ENGLISH ABOUT KOREA

Unit 1 KOREA IN BRIEF

I'd like to tell you something about Korea briefly.

As you know, Korea is divided into two parts; the Communist North Korea and the Democratic South Korea. The 38th Parallel was drawn when Korea was liberated from Japanese rule in 1945.

The area of the Korean Peninsula covers about 220,000 square kilometers or about 86,000 square miles. The area of the South Korea is slightly smaller than that of the North Korea. Korea is about the size of the State of New York of America or Great Britain.

It has the population of about 60 million altogether North and South, but the South has about 40 million people.

You may think that Korea is a new country which was born only a few decades ago. But it was founded more than 43 centuries ago. At the beginning of the Christian Era in Western Nations, there were three rival kingdoms in the Korean Peninsula. They are called Silla, Paekje, and Koguryo. The Silla Kingdom unified the three kingdoms in the 7th century within about the same boundary as that of today. The succeeding Koryo Dynasty lasted from the 10th to the 14th century. And then, we had the last kingdom named Yi Dynasty.

Japanese colonized and annexed Korea in 1910, ruling until the end of World War II in 1945. The government in the South Korea was established in 1948. Only two years later we had to go through the destructive Korean War begun in 1950 by a surprise attack from the Communist North Korea. With assistance from 16 U.N. member nations, the invasion was defeated and the border re-established.

Right after the Korean War we really had a hard time to recover the war-torn land. However, all the Koreans have worked very hard and have emphasized on modernization, industrialization, and economic development.

And it has resulted in a great progress for past 40 years. Many industrialized countries gave voice to admiration and concern over the miraculous economic development in recent years. So Korea is now one of the promising developing countries and trying to be one of the advanced countries in the near future.

Unit 2 HANGUL(The Korean Alphabet)

The Korean Language belongs to the Ural-Altaic language group which include Mongolian and Finnish. Called 'Hangul,' Korean character system is totally different from and completely independent of Chinese and Japanese. Invented by a group of scholars under the patronage of King Sejong in 1443, Hangul is composed of 10 vowels and 14 consonants -- 24 phonetic signs with which we are able to describe all the possible sounds. Korean writing is a good example of alphabetic system with symbols that do not resemble those of the Latin alphabet used in English (Linguistics Across Cultures: Robert Lado).

Korean written symbols represented sounds much as English writing does. In fact, Korean writing is more consistent in its representation of sounds than English. As we write almost the same way we pronounce, spelling in Korean is much easier than any other characters as far as I know. Thanks to its scientific syllabic system, it allows great freedom of expression. The English speaker learning to write Korean has to learn to write the symbols of the Korean alphabet as a separate undertaking, a problem that does not exist between English and Spanish.

Unit 3

EDUCATIONAL SYSTEM IN KOREA

Compared to the other countries in the Far East, school attendance rate and educational standard are very high here in Korea. Koreans are very enthusiastic about education.

The school system of Korea is characterized by six years of elementary school which is compulsory, three years of junior high, three years of senior high school and four years of college or university.

Besides the ordinary universities there are two year junior colleges and six year medical colleges. Teachers for elementary school are trained at four year's university of education.

The number of elementary school children today is about six million while high school enrollees are one million.

The ratio in public school and private school is 43% to 57%.

Thirty four per cent of senior high school graduates go to institutions of higher learning, tertiary education every year.

Korea's schools are operated on a two semester basis. The first semester lasts from March through the end of August and the second from September through the close of February the next year.

T : What kinds of schools are here and how many years in each school?

G : There is kindergarten which is not compulsory. One enters elementary school which is compulsory when one becomes six years of age. After elementary school comes junior high, so called "middle school" which has three years. And then senior high, we call it "high school," has three years. After high school comes college or university. Of course, there is also junior college which has two years.

T : I see.

T : What types of schools are here?

G : There are two types of schools. One is a public school and the other is a private school.

This is true from the lower school up to the university. Although the majority of the students are attending public elementary schools, the children of wealthy families are sent to private institutions for their primary education: and then secondary, public or private by lottery system. After finishing senior high, they mostly enter private universities or colleges for their tertiary education with a competitive entrance examination after taking a college entrance qualification test administered by the government.

In Korea government universities, we call them national universities, are considered superior to private universities.

Unit 4 MEETING AT INCHEON AIRPORT

Hello! Ladies and Gentlemen, welcome to the Land of Morning calm, the Republic of Korea.

My name is ___________, and I will be your tour guide during this brief an hour journey to your respective hotels.

We are now leaving Incheon Airport, the gateway to Korea. It is located 55 km west of Seoul, the Capital.

Incheon Int'l Airport is a threshold of Seoul which is the center of politics, economy, industry and culture. Seoul has been the capital city of our country since 1392 when the founder-king of the new Kingdom of Chosôn or Yi Dynasty moved the capital to Seoul.

At this time we are passing by the Han River. It is the 2nd longest river in Korea and provides the main water supply to the citizens of Seoul.

The Han River which we call Han-gang has played a very important role in the history of the Korean peninsula from ancient times.

This area has been inhabited from as early as 4000 B.C. as evidenced by the recent excavation of sites of prehistoric dwellings on the eastern outskirts of Seoul. The first capital city of the Paekche Kingdom, one of the three ancient kingdoms, was also located in the Seoul area, until the kingdom was driven south by the powerful Koguryo in the north.

We could be able to see canals and excursion ships plying the river after 1986. Also, larger recreational parks have been developed along the deserted river basin. Millions of trees will provide cool shade and add picturesque beauty to the city. After the 86 Asian Games, Seoul be came a city of comfort and pleasant ambience.

The domed structure over there is the National Assembly Building of Korea. It is regarded as the largest among its counterparts in Asia. It was completed in 1975 and took six years to construct its traditional Korean architecture, It is modeled of the Renaissance. The National Assembly of Korea adopts a unicameral legislature system and the tenure of office of the members is four years.

This building stands as a symbol of parliamentarism, public census, civil rights and the national solidarity for the essential reunification of our divided country.

Unit 5 KYEONGBOK PALACE

Seoul was the capital city during the 519 years of the Yi Dynasty, also called the Chosun Dynasty.

For most people today historic Seoul means the palaces of the capital. They are reminders of the splendor of the past dynasty, they offer pleasant parks for an afternoon's leisure, and they offer to Korean and foreign visitors alike a glimpse of the exotic, a peep into the pleasurable side of the life of the old royal court.

The plan of the palace derived from the Chinese plan, which hinged on the Chinese conception of kingship. This is that the King rules by the mandate of heaven and is the mediator between heaven and earth. The Chinese emperor considered himself the son of heaven and responsible to the whole earth.

We are now facing the Kwanghwa-mun(MUN means gate). It has a mythical beast named "Haetae", which was placed there to protect the palace from danger such as fire. It has been said that these beasts can tell good from evil and can destroy all evil. The female beast has her mouth open while the male's mouth is shut.

We are now entering the Kyeongbok Palace, the Palace of Shining Happiness. It was first built in 1392 by the founder King Taejo to be the residence and center of dynastic power of the Yi family.

At that time only royal persons like kings, queens and their courtiers were allowed to enter the palace.

In the past over 500 buildings were encompassed here, but most of them were burned during the Japanese invasion of 1592. Only ten of the buildings are still left. Despite this, the Kyôngbok Palace still retains its serenity and magnificent beauty.

The silhouette of superimposed brackets between huge posts and the ceiling is most spectacular. The excellent technique of building up the bracket complex without using a single, nail is nowhere employed so elaborately as in Kyôngbok Palace. The bracket system is to elevate the ceiling, and each bracket unit consists of three tiers while a fourth tier is added for the interior.

In the center of the rear half of the building is the throne platform, painted red, with a flight of five steps leading up to it. The throne is topped by a wooden canopy.

Unit 6

TÔKSU PALACE

Two or three minutes' walk from the Chosun Hotel to the west, the visitor arrives at the City Hall Square, and across the motor road running between the South Gate and the Capitol-Building, will see at the corner of the National Information Center a large red gate known as Taehanmun. On entering the gate, the visitor comes to a group of Korean style palace buildings on one side and the European style granite palace at the far end of the royal grounds, and the new Art Museum where an interesting collection of old porcelain, jewels, paintings, and calligraphy are on display.

The Korean style palaces were previously the residence of Princess Ôm(Ômbi), and when additional halls were erected, the Old Emperor(Kojong) moved his household here in February 1897 from the Russian Legation, where he had taken refuge for twelve months following his escape from the North Palace.

In January 1919, the Old Emperor died at his living chamber, Hamnyongjôn (Hall of All Peace), surrounded by peony gardens, in the Tôksu Palace. As he was forced to abdicate in 1907 at the point of Japanese bayonets, and then died of mysterious causes on the Eve of the Versailles Peace Conference, his sudden death fanned more anti-Japanese feeling among the Korean people, who rose up in the Independence Movement of March 1, 1919. The tens of thousands of demonstrators mourned the Emperor's death while they shouted Mansei! Long Live Korea! Inside the palace his royal body was lying in state.

Unit 7 PIWON(The Secret Garden)

This garden, occupying the northeastern portion of the palace is popularly known as Piwon or the Secret Garden, but its formal name was Rear Garden, North Garden or "Kumwon" meaning Forbidden Garden.

This garden originated in April of 1406, during the reign of King Taejong who erected numerous buildings in the palace. About six months after the completion of the buildings, the king built a beautiful pavilion and a lotus pond for the purpose of garden parties and Buddhist rituals of lantern viewing. The garden facilities were continually expanded.

Therefore, this garden provided successive kings with a place to rest in their busy life carrying out state affairs.

The garden has many pavilion buildings built to match the respective terrain and surroundings.

However, none of the buildings some sexogonal and others octogonal. They are roofed with tiles, some sexogonal and others octogonal. They are roofed with tiles, straw or bark depending on their-environs.

In other words, this garden is one vast museum of Korean architecture, gardening arts and historical tradition.

It sprawls over an area of nearly 50 acres comprising beautiful foothills and clear streams. Six lotus ponds and 28 pavilions of various size and type were built to blend in with the springs and woods.

Unit 8 NAMDAEMUN(The South Gate)

Of the four major gates and four other minor gates of ancient Seoul, the South Gate or the Gate of Respecting Rites is the most spectacular and majestic. Through this gate marched kings, princes, ambassadors and triumphant generals. This gate was indeed the symbol of the kingdom next only to Kyôngbok Palace. It has been designated National Treasure No. 1.

It was built between 1395 and 1398. The present edifice was built in 1447 during the reign of King Sejong, and is the oldest wooden building in Seoul. The Gate originally constituted the main entrance to the capital leading straight to Kyôngbok Palace through the Kwanghwa-mun Gate.

Its arch was the main entrance to the capital and great walls, twenty feet high, stood on either side. When the big bell in the heart of the city rang out the curfew, the gate was closed and traffic stopped. This city walls have gradually been removed and broad paved roads laid in their place. Remnants of them still exist on the mountain slopes nearby. The great arch of dressed stone through which those entering the city passed, support the superstructure. The gate was supported by a total of 22 round wooden columns -- 14 outer pillars, four inner pillars, and four central pillars. The gracefully curved lines of the double eaves and the rich bracket system give the imposing structure a feminine beauty. This gate was open for traffic until 1908 when the two roads were constructed outside the gate.

Unit 9

YONGIN NATURAL FARMLAND

The Yongin Natural Farmland occupies an area of 45 sq km and is often called “Family Land” because it is a family resort in the outskirts of Seoul where every member of the family can enjoy the facilities. Family Land is famous for its lion safari - the first of its kind in Korea and also includes a Natural Zoological Park, a Botanical Garden and an Amusement Park.

There are opportunities to watch magnificent performances of peacocks spreading their pompous rainbow colored wings, and to observe wild boars and exotic flamingos. Yongin Family Land boasts more than 4,500 varieties of animals grazing in the natural pasture ground.

In the Children’s Amusement Park there are many carnival rides, a magic house and a roller coaster. A visit to the folk art chamber in the Cultural Center is strongly recommended. Yongin is a place for all ages.

Unit 10

KOREAN FOLK VILLAGE
(Minsokchon)

Ladies and Gentlemen!

We have now arrived at the Korean Folk Village. I am glad that we have the opportunity to show you the 19th century Korea. In the Folk Village you will see more than 260 traditional Korean houses used for government offices, a weaving yard, a blacksmith's shop, houses of the high-ranking officials and peasant houses. These houses were all recreated from the original structures that have undergone the process of dismantling and restructuring. Opened at 1974, the Folk Village since then has become the most popular place for tourists.

CHANGSÔNG

Those two wooden faten poles you see over there are guardian deitys which the ancient Korean people firmly worshiped as a protection deity of the village. According to our historical record, it appeared about 2,000 years ago at an entrance to a village. We call these poles 'changsong' and they are also used as mileposts for travellers.

Unit 11

KYÔNGJU & POMUN LAKE BESORT

1. Kyôngju

Kyôngju City, the old capital of Silla Kingdom, is located about 260 miles (365km) southeast of Seoul, and it takes about five hours by bus from Seoul.

It is my great pleasure to show you around Kyôngju, which is our representative cultural city.

The area of Kyôngju covers about 214 square kilometers, and has a population of about 130,000. Kyôngju is called a museum without walls, filled with remains of the ancient Silla Kingdom.

Since Kyôngju was the capital of Korea during the Silla Dynasty (57 B.C. – 935 A.D.), this city is the brillant Silla Kingdom's remains.

The art and culture of Silla were unique and splendid; they had a sense of the essential harmony between man and nature, and used their technical skill with aesthetic sensitively.

There are two outstanding treasures in Kyôngju.

One is the Pulguksa Temple, and the other is Sôkuram Grotto. Sôkuram stands on the crest of Mt. Toham. It was built in the middle of the 8th century by the same architect who built Pulguksa Temple.

There are many other attractions such as tumuli park,

where General Kim Yushin Tomb, Astromonical Observatory (Chômsôngdae) and Pomun Lake Resort.

The magnificent shape of the remains of the walls on the hills surrounding the ancient capital, the ancient tombs that look just like small hills, temples, golden crowns, stone pagodas, Buddhist statues, temple bells, fragments of tiles--all seem to speak vividly of the past splendor.

2. POMUN LAKE RESORT

Now here we are at Pomun Lake Resort.

You can go for or stroll around this lovely resort or buy some souvenirs all afternoon.

We are going to stay here until five o'clock. This resort covers about 2,600 acres and it is surrounded by wooded mountains, lending the entire region an atmosphere of peace and tranquility in harmony with natural beauty and rich antiquity.

The banks of the lake slope gently up over rolling hills to the very foot of the mountain.

Along the western hills the ancient ruins of Myônghwal Mountain Fortress are still seen.

These walls date to the 5th century. Near the shores are two large reconstructed three-storied pagodas which date to the Unified Silla Period.

The lake is fed by the Pukch'ôn (North Stream) and drains off into the Hyôngsan River.

Our government has developed this resort to expand the international tourist market.

We have tried to restore and preserve the original beauty and authenticity of the historic Silla remains.

Unit 12

SEORAKSAN NATIONAL PARK (Snow Mountain)

In the northeast corner of the Republic's territory, a chain of mountains begins which stretch north across the border into Communist-held territory, where its loftiest peaks have been known immemorially as the Diamond Mountains, acclaimed as the most impressive scenery on the entire peninsula.

The southern spurs of this range, much more than mere chips of the diamond, are called Seoraksan, which is today a national park under active development as a resort.

Outer Seorak, as the resort district is called, lies quite close to the fishing port of Sokcho. A great many hotels, large and small, have been added recently to the amenities of the area as well as inns of varying size and quality.

Advance reservations should be made in the peak travel seasons of spring and fall.

As the valley road winds its way toward the Seorak tourist village, imposing mountain ramparts loom ever more loftily ahead, their steepness making them appear even higher.

Some climbers do indeed go "over the top," and even come down on the other side - a two-day hike, but most visitors content themselves with the safer thrills of a cable car that soars airily in 20 minutes high above trails that those below struggle for hours to traverse.

It is an altogether easier choice to follow the main road out the other end of the bustling tourist village and over a footbridge, after which the path divides.

Close-by is Uisang-dae pavilion, built on the site that monk Uisang frequented many years ago. Sunrises draw large numbers of visitors; a most beautiful setting among ancient pine trees and sea-mist which rises only to be dispersed shortly by sunrise.

Unit 13 TONGDOSA TEMPLE

Now we are passing through the Tongdosa Temple area, which is one of the three largest temples in Korea.

Tongdosa Temple was founded in 646 under the reign of Queen Sôndok by a Buddhist priest Jajang. For 1300 years from then on, the temple bell has been rung at a given time every day without fail. The bell ringing out throughout the valley is not just an ordinary metallic sound but touching message of salvation which tells Buddha's will to deliver mankind.

What makes this temple different from others is that there is no Buddhist statue in the inner temple. It is because this temple has a special sacristy for Buddha's sarira, the relics of Buddha, just behind the main temple. People pray and perform rituals for this sarira instead of the image of Buddha. Tongdosa Temple comprises thirty-five buildings including the main temple together with stone pagodas, stone lanterns, fragrant braziers, and it keeps a 1300 year-old surplice which is said to be worn by the priest Jajang. Now 100 odd monks are staying here, and twelve hermitages in the mountains behind the temple serve as places for ascetic practices.

Unit 14

CHEJU TOUR

Cheju Island is located 165 miles off the southern port of Pusan and is an oval shaped island measuring forty-one kilometers across from north to south and 73 kilometers across from east to west.

This is Korea's only island province and has a population of 519,000. On account of its geographical location and adjoining warm oceanic current, the island enjoys mild weather all the year round. The plants and landscape are entirely different from those of the mainland.

Because of its volcanic origin, the island is short of natural water supplies. Therefore the main products of the island are day crops, tangerines and fish stuffs.

One of the famed features of the island is the women divers who make their living gathering sea food and other marine products from the depths of the ocean even in winter.

From ancient time Cheju has been called the island of the three riches referring to the abundance of rocks, wind and women. Nowadays, the island is praised for its 'three lacks' thieves, gates and beggars.

It is popular as a tourist destination for summer and winter vacationers. Good hotels and recreational facilities are available on the island. It is easily accessible by air and boat.

ANNOUNCEMENT

Your attention, please. Korean Airlines announces the departure of the Flight 427 to Cheju Island. Flight 427 is now boarding at Gate 3. All passengers aboard please. Thank you.

Your attention, please. Korean Airlines Flight 427 is now ready for departure at Gate 3. All aboard, please. This is a final call. Thank you.

Good afternoon, ladies and gentlemen. Korean Airlines welcomes you aboard the Flight 427, nonstop to Cheju Island. Our flying time will be one hour and 20 minutes. We expect to arrive at Cheju Airport at three- thirty, Korea Standard Time. Please fasten your seat-belt and observe the no-smoking sign. Thank you.

Ladies and Gentlemen! You may now unfasten your seatbelt and relax. If we can be of any help to you during the flight, just press the call button directly above you.

We are Flying at an altitude of 25,000 feet at a ground speed of 450 miles per hour. The weather forecast for Korea calls for fair skies and warm temperature for today, light wind northeast.

Temperature in the Cheju area now is 75 degrees by the Fahrenheit.

Skies will be fair tonight with increased cloudness.

Light rain is forecast for the central and northern section of the nation tomorrow.

Tonight's temperature is expected to be a low of 50 degrees near the capital and a high of 70 degrees by the Fahrenheit. Along the south coast and Cheju area 70 degrees, and 80 degrees are expected highs. It's 2:30 Korea Standard Time. Thank you.

It's 20 minutes before we reach Cheju Airport. Introducing the island, Cheju is the only island province of Korea located in the southern sea of the peninsular. It's an oval shaped island with a population of 200,000.

It measures 41 kilometers across from North to South and 73 km across from East to West.

The island enjoys a semitropical climate with mild weather all year round but because of its volcanic origin, the island is short of natural water supplies.

Mt. Halla is the highest mountain with a highest of 1,952 meters and is famous for its good hiking course.

The main products of the island are tangerines and fish stuffs.

The women divers are well known tourist attractions and there are many good resort spots for summer sportsmen and anglers as well as golfers. Thank you.

Stewardess : Are you comfortable?

Tourist : Yes, thank you.

S : If you want anything, will you press the call button?

T : ...... (pushes the button)

S : Yes, sir. What can I do for you?

T : Yes, I'd like something to read. Do you have any magazines or newspapers.

S : Yes, we have some. This is Newsweek Korea Times.

T : Thank you.

S : Anything you care for, sir?

T2 : Just a glass of water, please.

S : I will bring it right away, sir.

T : Thank you.

Korean Airlines announces the departure of the Flight 427 to Cheju Island.

Flight 427 is now ready for departure at Gate 3.

Our flight time will be one hour and 20 minutes.

Please fasten your seat-belt. If we can be of any help to you, just press the call button.

We are flying at an altitude of 25,000 feet.

Light rain is forecast for the northern section of the nation.

Tonight's temperature is expected to be a low of 50 degrees near the capital.

It's 20 minutes before we reach Cheju.

PART VII

INTERVIEW ENGLISH

Unit 1 ABOUT YOURSELF

A : Good afternoon. Can I have your name, please?

B : My name is Sunny Lee.

A : When were you born?

B : I was born on January 29th, 1979.

A : How old are you?

B : I am twenty-four years old.

A : Is there any relatives in the United States?

B : No, there isn't. But some of my friends live in New York./ Yes, my cousin lives in L.A.

A : Are you married?

B : No, I am single.

A : What do you do for a living?

B : I'm with the Bank of Korea. /I am working for a trading company in Seoul as a manager of development department.

A : Who finances your expenses? / Who is your financial sponsor?

B : My father in Seoul does. / My father is.

A : Who will pay for the registration fee?

B : My father in Seoul will pay for it.

A : Who pays for your boarding and food?

B : It's my own expenses. My father pays for tuition only.

A : What is your nationality?

B : I'm Korean.

Unit 2

AMBITIONS AND ASPIRATIONS & SPECIAL QUALIFICATIONS

(Applying for a Job)

A : What made you choose this company?

B : Working in this company would give me the best chance to use what I've learned in university, studying tourism hotel and travel agency administration for four years.

A : What is your philosophy?

B : I think sincerity is the best policy. Whatever occupation one may engage in, he must do his best.

A : Tell me what you think a job is?

B : Well, a way to make a living, of course, but beyond that I think works are ways of developing as a person.

A : What do you think is the most important thing for happiness for you?

B : I think the most important thing is having and making good friends. A person can't live by himself.

A : Do you have any licenses or other special qualifications?

B : I have a driver's license.

A : I want to know if you have any special skills?

B : I've passed the tests of overseas escort. /I've passed the tests of business skills for abacus.

A : What are your qualifications for being a stenographer?

B : I can type sixty words per minute and I take shorthand at eighty words per minute.

Unit 3 MAJOR SUBJECT

A : What is your major?

B : I specialized in tourism administration.

A : If you enter this company what section would you like to work in?

B : I'd like to work in the outbound section. /I'd like to work as a front cashier.

A : If you were to work for this company, how much do you expect to get a month?

B : Well, that's a tough question to answer. Of course the more, the better. But I believe that I can get seven hundred and fifty dollars a month.

A : Do you have any question you would like to ask me?

B : May I ask how much the bonuses are?

A : We pay 400% annual bonus. Does this satisfy you?

B : I am perfectly satisfied.

A : How many years have you worked in this field?

B : I've worked for three years in this field.

A : What basic principle do you follow in your life?

B : Do not put off till tomorrow what can be done today.

Unit 4

MOTIVATION TO STUDY ABROAD

A : Why do you want to study in the United States?

B : Because my friend who has been studying for a long time in the States invited me.

A : What is you purpose in applying for a visa?

B : I want to study tourism administration at University of Hawaii.

A : When did you graduate from university?

B : I graduated from university last year.

A : Have you taken TOEFL?

B : Yes, I have. I scored 600.

A : Would you mind telling me what kind of grades you have?

B : Of course not. My grades weren't very good. I spent all my time on club activities, and missed a lot of classes.

A : Do you think your English is good enough to study in an American university?

B : I guess I can do it well.

A : After graduation in the U.S. what will you do?

B : I'll return to Korea and I want to teach students in Korea. /I want to get a job as a travel agent.

A : After college, what do you want to do?

B : I want to do graduate work in a school of education.

A : How long are you going to stay in the U.S.?

B : It will take at least five years.

Unit 5 TO EMIGRATE

A : Why do you intend to emigrate to the United States?

B : Because I want to educate my children in the United States.

A : What are you going to do in the States?

B : I'm going to work as a cook.

A : How many family members do you have?

B : I have five members, sir./There are five(members) in my family.

A : Good luck to you.

- 사증면접(visa interview)은 해당 입국할 국가의 영사가 여행 목적을 수행할 적임자인가 확인하고 사증을 발급하기 위하여 면접을 하는데 이민(Immigration)과 비이민(Non-immigration), 더 세분해서 각 목적별로 다음 사항에 유익해야 한다.
  ① 사증신청서와 초청장의 내용과 일치하는 답변을 할 것.
  ② 비 이민자가 영주할 의사를 표시해서는 안되고 직장을 가질 의사를 말해도 안된다.
  ③ 이민자의 경우는 물론 영주와 취업의사를 사실대로 진술할 것.
  ④ 당황하지 말고 침착하며 한편 예의 범절을 지켜 명랑한 분위기를 조성할 것.
  ⑤ 모르는 것은 서슴치 말고 반문해야 하며 이때 「"I beg your pardon, sir?"」 또는 "I beg your pardon, ma'am?"(뭐라고 말씀하셨는지요?)라고 공손하게 표현해야 한다.

- 출국 준비
  해외여행을 위해서는
  A ① 여권(Passport)의 신청
  ② 비자(Visa)의 신청
  ③ 전염병 예방접종증명서(International Vaccination Certificate)의 신청
  ④ 외화 구입 신청 등의 수속 절차를 마치는 일
  B 비행기 표 사는 일
  C 호텔을 예약하는 일 등이 꼭 필요한데 이런 일들은 단체 여행이면 주최자 측에서 해 주며, 또 여행 대리점(Travel Agent)에 개인적으로 부탁해도 수속을 모두 해 준다.
  이러한 준비 중 행선지에서 rent-a-car(전세차)를 이용하기 위하여 「국제운전면허증(International Driving Permit)」의 교부수속도 해 두는 것이 좋다.

Unit 6 JOB INTERVIEW

A : Let me ask you a few questions. Where do you live?
B : I live in An-yang.
A : And what school are you attending?
B : I attend Seoul College.
A : Where is that?
B : I beg your pardon?
A : Where is Seoul College located?
B : Oh, it's at 731 Hwagok-dong, Seoul, sir.
A : And what is your major?
B : I'm majoring in English.
A : Have you ever worked in an office before?
B : Yes, I had a part-time job for two months at Samhwa Trading Company.
A : What did you do there?
B : Mostly typing and running errands, sir.
A : Have you ever been overseas?
B : Yes, I've been to the United States. I have lived in New York for one year.
A : Have you studied English typing?
B : Yes, sir. I have studied English typing.
A : What are your hobbies? /What do you like to do in your spare time?

B : Well, I like reading, and listening to music – especially American folk songs. I play the guitar a little, and I like the movies, too.

A : What do you like best about school?

B : The oral English classes. We get a lot of chances to speak English.

A : Why did you choose this company? / What made you choose this company?

B : Well, I know that you do a very big internal business, so I thought it would be a good place for me to use the experience.

A : Very glad to have met you. We'll be letting you know the result of the interview sometime next week. Thank you very much for coming in.

B : Thank you very much for giving me your time.

A : You're quite welcome. Good-bye.

B : Good-bye.

Unit 7

TOUR GUIDE & OVERSEAS ESCORT

1. Will you introduce yourself to me? /Tell me a little about yourself.

2. What's your name? /Can I have your name, please?

3. What's your application number?
/My application number is 2102, sir.

4. What school did you graduate from?/What is your educational background? I graduated from Hanyang University.

5. What's your major?
(1)I majored in English.
(2) My major is Tourism.

6. Can you tell me what school you are attending and what's your major?

7. Why are you majoring in Tourism? /Why did you apply for a guide liscense?

8. What have you been doing since graduation? I have been studying for the exam of English Tour Guide.

9. Where are you working now? /What do you do for a living? I'm working for Seoul Trading Company.

10. Where are you from? /I'm from Pusan.

11. What is your home town famous for?

12. How large is your family? /There are five in my family.

13. What are the most important things to be a good tour guide? /What do you think the essential elements are in being a guide?

14. What does your father do?

15. Where do you live now?

16. When will you graduate?

17. How many national parks are there in Korea?

18. How many palaces are there in Seoul?

19. What is the second largest city in Korea?

20. What's the population of Seoul?

21. What's the population of Korea?

22. What kinds of food do you eat on Chusok?

23. What kinds of food do you eat during the new year holidays?

24. What's the most popular spectator sport in Korea?

25. How many foreign tourists visited last year?

26. What is the name of the most famous shopping center (street) in Seoul ?

27. When was Buddhism introduced into Korea?

28. When was Christianity introduced into Korea?

29. What are famous hot springs in Korea?

30. What are the chief English newspapers published in Korea? Do you read any English papers?

31. I want to buy some Korean souvenirs. What would you recommend?

32. I want to see the typical and traditional Korean way of life and customs. Where should I go?

33. When do you observe Hangul Day?

34. How long does it take from here to Kyongju by train?

35. Can you tell me something about Ginseng?

36. Would you explain how to use chop-sticks?

37. Would you explain about Korean food?

38. I want to do some shopping. Where should I go?

39. I want to do sightseeing tour in Seoul for two days. Could you give me some suggestions?

40. What is the National Treasure No. 2 ?

41. What does KNTC stand for?

42. How long does it take to get to Chejudo by air?

43. What kinds of tourism are there in Korea?

44. What is your biggest hope in the future?

45. How many foreign tourists visit Korea annually? More than 5 million people visit Korea annually. Last year 5,150,000 tourists visited Korea.

46. What does I.O.C. stand for? It stands for International Olympic Committee.

47. What does K.O.C. stand for? It means Korean Olympic Committee.

48. Where is the Head Office of I.O.C. located? It's located in Laussane in Switzerland.

49. How many countries took part in the Seoul Olympic Games? One hundred sixty countries took part in the games.

50. How many members took part in it ? Approximately thirty seven thousand members did.

51. How many foreign tourists visited '88 Seoul Olympic Games ? About two hundred thousand people.

52. What does ASTA stand for? It stands for American Society of Travel Agents.

53. What does PATA stand for? It stands for Pacific Asia Travel Association.

54. What's WTO? It means World Tourism Organization.

55. What's EATA? It means East Asia Travel Association.

56. What are the three most beautiful ports in the world? They're Naples, Rio de Janeiro and Sydney.

57. What are the most famous sightseeing places in Southeast Asia? They're Hongkong, Macao, Bangkok, Singapore and Bali Island.

58. What are the most famous sightseeing places in Japan? They're Kyoto historical spot. Volcanic hot springs in Kyusyu District.

59. What's IPU? It means the Inter-Parliamentary Union.

60. What was the first hotel in Korea? It was Sontak Hotel.

61. Please explain something about the effect of tourism. We can obtain foreign currency, the international goodwill, cultural inter-change, the enhancement of our country's prestige and the best use in leisure.

62. What are the most famous sightseeing places in the United States? They're Niagara Falls, Disney Land, Miami Beach.

63. What is the most sparsely-populated country? It's the Commonwealth of Australia.

64. What is the longest river in the world? It's the Nile.

65. What are the most famous sightseeing places in the world? They're the Alps, Florida, Monaco, Paris and Niagara Falls.

66. What is the Worid Tourist Day? It's September 28th.

67. What country gets the highest tourist income in the Orient? It's Singapore, she gets the highest tourist income in the Orient.

68. What country gets the highest tourist income in the worid? It's Spain or Italy.

69. What does C.I.Q. stand for? It means Customs, Immigration and Quarantine, sir.

70. What does a tour guide do? Tour guide means the person in charge of a tour and who accompanies a sightseeing trip.

71. What qualities does a sightseeing guide need? A sightseeing guide needs two qualities – an outgoing personality and language skill. In other words, he needs the qualities of a diplomat.

72. What does ETA stand for? It stands for Estimated Time of Arrival.

73. What does ETD mean? It means Estimated Time of Departure.

74. Could you tell me about your personal history briefly? I graduated from Kangwon National University in 1999. My major was Tourism Management. And I'm going to be an Interpreter (Tour Guide).

75. What is American Plan? It means the system of charges including room, all meals at a hotel.

76. What is Eurailpass?

It is a railroad ticket to provide unlimited 1st class rail travel throughout 17 countries of Western Europe. Fares are flat rates for specified number of days.

77. What is European Plan (EP)?

It is hotel accommodations with no meals included in the cost of the room.

78. What does Great Britain consist of?

It consists of England, Wales, Scotland and Northern Ireland. The country is called the United Kingdom(the U.K.).

79. What does a convention mean?

It means a meeting at which people usually within the same field or business exchange their ideas, experiences, specialized knowledge, and so on.

80. What is IATA?

It stands for the International Air Transport Association, a voluntary association of international airlines. It sets fares and other standards for most airlines service by agreement.

81. Definition of Tourism

Tourism is defined as all activities outside of the home community except daily commuting to and from work regardless of distance traveled, destination, origin, or mode of transportation.

The purpose of the trip is unimportant; it can be pleasure, business, convention, personal or any other reason.

82. Passport

The passport is a formal document issued by a competent officer of a country to a citizen of the country and now usually necessary for exit from and reentry into the country, that certifies to the identity and citizenship of the bearer, calls upon the officers of foreign governments to extend protection to him when needed, and allows him to travel within the borders of a foreign country when it has been endorsed with a visa by an authorized official of that country.

When you're traveling, your passport is worth more than gold.

83. Visa

Visa is, in effect a stamp of approval put into your passport which declares that this document has been examined and found in order for passage to the country granting the visa.

It is your permission to enter that country and is the reason a passport carries several blank pages marked visa. You can apply for a visa at the Consulate or Embassy of the country in question.

When required

All aliens who want to travel to Korea must obtain a visa from a Korean embassy or consulate. There are three kinds of visas: the tourist visa, the transit visa and the entry visa.

Tourist Visa: This visa is issued to aliens whose purpose of entry is sightseeing and the period of stay is within 60 days. It can be obtained when a round trip ticket is shown and application is submitted to a Korean embassy or consulate.

Transit Visa: This visa is issued to aliens who pass through Korea in order to go to a third country from their own, or vice versa, and the period of stay is for 15 days. Application procedures are the same as those for a tourist visa.

Entry Visa: This visa is issued to aliens who want to enter Korea for purposes other than tourism or transit. The period of stay varies depending on the status of entry. Application for this visa must be submitted to a Korean embassy or consulate together with the documents required according to the desired status of entry.

84. Tourist Attractions

Definition of tourist attractions is anything that attracts tourists and it can be just about anything and they are an important part of tourism.

There are three kinds of attractions. One is natural beauty, as represented by Grand Canyon, Yellowstone National Park, etc. The next one is man-made attractions. Among man-made attractions that lead in popularity are San Francisco's Golden Gate Bridge, Mount Rushmore etc. The third one is events, Olympic Games, boxing matches, etc.

85 Factors Affecting Travel

The most important factors affecting tourism are a) increasing discretionary time b) greater disposable income c) relative cost of travel d) higher educational level e) larger percentage of young adults, and f) changing life styles that inlcude travel as an important part of living.

86. Travel Agent's Job

Travel agent's job description would include the following tasks;

a) to organize all kinds of tours and sells prepared package tour.

b) to arrange of the components of tourism such as hotels, motels, etc.

c) to handle and advise on the many details involved in modern day travel, e.g.: travel and baggage insurance and traveler's checks, etc.

d) to use professional know-how and experience. It is information which the traveler can spend days or weeks of endless phone calls, letters and visits to secure, and still may not get it right.

e) to arrange reservations for special–interest activities –religious pilgrimages, and sporting trips.

87. WTO (the World Tourism Organization) was formed as a successor to IUOTO in November, 1974 for the purpose of promoting and developing tourism in the interest of economic, social, and cultural progress of all nations.

88. PATA (Pacific Asia Travel Association): Membership organization of govemment and private business representatives that seeks to promote and monitor travel to and within the Pacific Asia.

89. ASTA (American Society of Travel Agents): Trade association of the United States travel agents and tour operators. International and allied memberships for trade-associated industries are also offered.

APPENDIX

1 영문, 이력서, 응시원서, 청구서, 추천서 예문
2 영문사용의 유의점(어법 및 발음)
3 호텔종사원 및 관광통역안내원 자격시험 영어 예상문제

APPENDIX 1.

Résumé

September 24, 2002

Name in Full: Changsoo Lee
Date of Birth: September 18, 1970 Sex: Male
Permanent Address: 34-2 Yongchon-dong, Sodaemoon-ku, Seoul, Korea
Present Address: 138-6 Shinsa-dong, Kangnam-ku, Seoul Telephone: 543-7337

Education:

- February 1990 Graduated from Daeshin Senior High School, Seoul
- March, 1990 Entered College of Education, Hanyang University, Seoul
- February 1994 Graduated from the above mentioned school
- February 2002 Received MBA at the above mentioned school.

Work Experiences:

- March 1994–February 1996: Taught at Hanyang Girls' Senior High School, Seoul
- May 1997–January 2000: Military Service
- June 2000–September 2002 : Worked for Hanson Trading Company, Seoul

Awards & Punishment:

Award－Awarded the second prize in the University English Speech Contest in November, 1993.

Punishment－None

I hereby certify that the above statements are true and correct to the best of my knowledge.

Changsoo Lee

※ 요즈음은 학력(education)과 경력(work experiences)은 최근의 것을 먼저 적는, 즉 연 연대순(reversed chronological order)으로 작성하는 것이 이상적이므로 적극 권장한다.

Model 1.

Asking the Application Form

April 24, 2003

Dear Sir:

I would like to study in the United States of America, I wish to enter your graduate school of Tourism Administration for Master's degree. I send all my credentials forward to you. Your prompt reaction will be highly appreciated.

Sincerely Yours,
Changsoo Lee

Model 2.

March 9, 2003

Dear Dr. William:

Having graduated from the Department of Business Administration at Hansung University in February, 2003 here in Seoul, I would like to apply for admission and a tuition scholarship at your University for the spring semester of 2004. I shall appreciate your sending me the necessary application forms for admission with financial support to your Department of Business Administration for a Master's Degree of Science.

As soon as I receive your letter, I shall forward you all my supporting documents. I am looking forward to your response at your earliest convenience.

Respectfully yours,
Changho Lee

Model 3.

Model Application Letter for Junior College Graduate

March 12, 2003

Dear Sir:

This letter is written in hopes that your University might be able to assist me in pursuing my educational career. Your undergraduate school has been highly recommended to me by my professors here.

I graduated from the Department of English at Hansung Junior College of Arts and Sciences in February, 2001- After graduation, I accepted a teaching position at the Sang-Kil Middle School, Seoul, and have remained in this position up to now.

Since my graduation from the college, I have been directing my energies toward the study of Special Education, and am hoping that I might be able to continue my research work and study at your University in the United States. I have successfully taken the TOEFL examination and wish to apply for a scholarship at your University for a bachelor's degree.

I request that you send me application forms or admission for either the spring or the fall semester of 2004. Any assistance you may be able to give me will be deeply appreciated, and I will forward references and academic transcripts when requested.

Sincerely yours,
Changsoon Lee

Model 1. Job

Letter of Recommendation

October 25, 2003

To Whom It May Concem:

It is with a great pleasure that I recommend Mr. Lee to your company.

Through my observation during the four year period I taught him at college, I can assure you that Mr. Lee is not only an ardent worker but also a trustworthy man. He has a marvelous command of practical English, both written and spoken, and also a strong sense of responsibility. And he is always agreeable and gets along well with other students.

I feel confident that he will prove an invaluable help to your company if you would employ him.

Changmoon Lee
Professor
Department of Tourism
Hanyang University

Model 2. Studying Abroad

Letter of Recommendation

April 21, 2003

Director of Graduate Studies
Dept. of Studio Arts
208 Art Building
216 21st Avenue South
Minneapolis, Minnesota 55455

Name in Full: Changsoon Lee
Date of Birth: September 14, 1978
Course ofStudy: Ceramic Arts
Nationality: Korean by birth
Date of Graduation: 1999 Undergraduate school from Department of Ceramic Arts, Fine Arts College, Hansung University, Seoul, Korea. 2003 Ceramic Arts major–Graduate School of Fine Arts, Hansung University, Seoul, Korea

Dear Sir:

It is with great pleasure that I recommend to you Miss Changsoon Lee who had been my student as a ceramic arts major at Hansung University, Seoul, Korea. I rarely recommend a student to a foreign university unless I am convinced that she will be able to perform well and be a credit to her country.

During her college and graduate school years from 1995–1999 she completed the course of ceramic arts under my supervision. I was favorably impressed with her diligence as well as her excellent marks. I'm deeply convinced that this young scholar should be encouraged and aided in continuing her education.

And she also has a very good command of English.

As her professor from 1995 to 1999 I feel myself qualified to comment on many aspects of her character. If you need any further information, please do not hesitate to ask me.

Sincerely yours,

Tongmin, Kim
Professor
Department of Ceramic Arts
Hansung University

APPENDIX 2.

Special areas of difficulty a Korean is likely to encounter in learning to speak, read & write English

1. The articles "a", "an", "the".

Short as these words are, if they are misused an English speaker would regard a person's English as being awkward, childish, or clumsy. In fact, a common way in Australia of parodying Aborigins and other primitive peoples has been to portray them as saying things like "I want apple." or "I like sky." instead of "I want an apple." and "I like the sky."

2. Plurals.

With a few minor exceptions like "sheep" and "fish," all countable nouns in English have a recognizable plural form the use of which is mandatory in any situation involving more than one of the objects, actions, or ideas the nouns refer to. (e.g.: I like apples. I have five dollars.)

3. Pronouns.

Pronouns like articles, are at the core of the English language. Using their forms properly should become an automatic processs to anyone who intends to develop a command of English.

4. Prepositions.

English employs far more prepositions than Korean does

and, unfortunately for people who want to learn the language, in many cases even a delicate choice of prepositions can be crucial to the meaning of an expression (e.g., "I'm looking for Elton" vs. "I'm looking at Elton" or "I'm looking to Elton," etc.)

5. "Yes/no", "come/go", "bring/take", "fetch."

These and similar words are widely used in English, just as their counterparts are in Korean. Unfortunately, though, they may represent different or even opposite concepts in one language than in the other and must therefore be used with caution. (For instance, the appropriate response to a statement like "Faith didn't come" should be "no" if one agrees with the speaker.)

(Are you coming to my place this evening? Yes, I'm coming./ No, I'm not coming.)

6. Verb Tenses.

There is an extensive range of verb tense forms in English. Some of these forms may carry overlapping or nearly identical meaning depending upon circumstances, but it is still safe to say that there are certain invariable relationships between these verb forms and points or periods in time which must be understood before a Korean can use English.

7. Auxiliary Verbs.

The forms of words like "can," "will," "shall," "may," "might" carry an enormous burden of meaning in English, and sentences will almost certainly be confusing if these words are omitted or misapplied.

8. Names.

By Korean standards, Western names are 'backward'? i.e., one's family name comes after one's given name rather than before it. Nearly everyone in Korea is aware of this fact, yet even among English teachers here probably no more than 50% are able consistently to call someone named "John A. Smith" what he should be called – either "Mr. Smith" or "John" without thinking about it.

9. Punctuation and Capitalization.

Rules of punctuation and capitalization in English may strike a Korean as being trivial or silly; indeed, many English speaking students struggling through classes with especially traditionally oriented English teachers feel the same way. But failing to observe these rules is much more dangerous for non-native than for an English speaker, because it may obscure meaning as well as merely affronting commaphiles and basic clues, determine many of the features of rhythm and even intonation in a given passage just by noticing which punctuation marks appear in and where.

10. Composition and Paragraphing.

In attempting to write English well, producing gramatically-sound, aesthetically-pleasing sentence is only half the battle. As in Korean prose, ideas have to be presented logically and sequentially if they are to have the impact one intends.

11. Spacing.

Hyphenating words and leaving the correct amount of space between them is a basic component of English writing. Properly executed, spacing is invisible to an English speaker but it is botched, the result will seem primitive or laughable to him.

12. Idioms.

Day-to-day English speech and writing norms are constantly and very rapidly changing. It is, therefore, extremely difficulty for a non-English speaker to keep his or her own English "contemporary." Fortunately, though, most Koreans have access to American television and radio through the armed forces broadcasting network. The more they can make use of this unique source of real English, the better; lists of idioms in most books, by contrast, are bound to be either antiquated, incomplete, or both.

13. Stress & Intonation

The same is true of English stress intonation as of its slang and idioms; there is no way to master them merely by reading books about them. Even the intonation rules which textbooks present as fundamental and ironclad are frequently bent or entirely disregarded by native speakers. On the other hand, to speak English without any concept of its typical melodies is to neglect one of its essential features and invite misunderstanding in conversation.

green hôuse red câp=a cap whose color is red

grêen house rêd cap=a baggage porter as at a railroad station

What are you working fôr? (=What are you trying to obtain?)

What are you wôrking for? (=Why are you working?)

They saw her dûck.

Some Principles of English Pronunciation

I. Aspirated(유기음이 될 때)

a) Initial /p.k.t./ pin pork paint time till key call kill cry
b) Accent right after /p.k.t/ appear atténd becóme Septémber compéte contáin occúr vacátion

2. Unaspirated(무기음이 될 때)

a) /p.k.t./ right after "s" still style skill spin steak school space stay skate speak speech
b) Accent right before /p.k.t./ ápple súccor cópy bútter círcus cápital láter tícket chícken

3. Fricative

a) Labio-dental /f/&/v/. fine fail half proof coffee fifty vine vale prove five
b) Dental fricatives /Θ/&/ð/. thin thick think thought they breathe bathe smooth mouths
c) Sibilant /s/&/z/. cease loose sink house race seas lose houses Mona Liza

4. Voicing(무성음의 유성음화) /t/ medial

bútter prétty fórty wáter báttery párty gét-away mótto Ítaly líttle tótal Put it on! Bétty gót a létter, not a sweater.
news−newspaper

What do you have to drink? Sit down. / sidaun/

5. Devoicing(유성음의 유성음화)

/ hǽftə /I have to study. You have to stay here./

/ hǽftu: /I don't want to, but I have to.

/ hǽvtu: /They have two rooms./ hǽstə /Dick has to study. She has to wash the dishes.

6. Assimilation(同化현상)

a) Progressive Assimilation: on the bus on the table on the answer sheet What's wrong?

b) Regressive Assimilation: this shoe this shape this shrimp

c) Reciprocal Assimilation: would you did you .could you meet you don't you

d) 뒤에 오는 nasal의 영향을 받을 때 submit footnote admire kidney nickname

7. Dissimilation(異化현상)

surprise / səpráiz / secretary / sέkəteri / library / laibəri /

8. Haplology(두개로 겹친 소리를 한번만 발음하는 현상)

Elision (생략) 또는 Contraction (축약) 현상

yes, sir good day next time madam-ma'am

humbley-humbly probably/-probly/ similarly / síməli /

/P-P/ You must stop playing. /t-t/ I went to town.

I like the shape of that table. She ate ten cookies.

/d-d/ He had done it. I saw a mad-dog. They could drive it.

/k-k/ a comic cartoon a public-career

/g-g/ We saw the big game. /f-f/ Take off four pounds. We'd laugh for an hour. /m-m/ It was the same man.

He became more at home. /v–v/ We love vegetables.
We drove very slowly. /s–s/ gas–station last–summer.
It makes some sense. They pass some cake.

9. Elision of Consonant(자음의 탈락)

a) is he / izi: / Is he upstairs? Is he leaving now? Where is he? Why is he going there?

b) was he / wə́zi: / Was he reading a book? When was he planning to see me? Was he expecting her?

c) has he / hǽzi: / Has he ever been to the States? Has he told her about it?

d) does he / dʌzi: / Does he have a dark blue book? Where does she planning to go? Does he understand it?

e) did he / didi: / Where did he want to go? Did he read the book?

f) know her / nouə / meet her / mí:tə / believe her / bilívə / Do you know her? Did you meet her? Can you believe her?

g) tell them / teləm / keep them send them
Plzease tell them. Please keep them. Please send them.

10. Liaison 연음

a) far away / fa:rəwei / It is your apple. / irizjuərǽpl /

b) There is no one here by that name.
You are wanted on the phone. I <u>want to</u> go home. I am <u>going to</u>+V... I <u>ought to</u> + V... / arə /

c) of / ə / a cup of coffee a glass of milk
a pound of sugar a ton of coal
Please give me a cup of coffee.
The doctor gave me a bottle of medicine.

Leave me alone.

I can go. You are wrong.

11. Initial Consonant Clusters

/ kr– / cry cross cream /gr–/ green great grand grade

/tr–/ try truck tree true train /dr–/ dream dry

/str–/ street straight strike /spr–/ spring spread spray

/skr-/ screen scratch /spl––/ split splash splendid splice

12. Clear "l" & dark "l".

a) Clear "l": love line lamp

b) Dark "l": help milk film well (l + consonant, l ending)

13. Tongue Twister

Peter Piper picked a peck of pickled peppers.

Fifty fowls with fluffy feathers.

She sells sea shells on the sea shore.

The swan swam over the sea and the swan swam well.

Once a fellow met a fellow in a field of beans.

APPENDIX 3.

호텔종사원 및 관광 통역 안내원 자격시험 영어예상문제

1. 밑줄 친 "a"의 발음이 다른 셋과 다른 것은?
   a) nature b) national c) declaration
   d) stationery e) education

2. 밑줄 친 "ch"의 발음이 다른 셋과 다른 것은?
   a) chauffeur b) stomachache c) chandelier
   d) moustache e) machinery

3. 다음중 제 1 accent(역점)의 위치가 잘못 표시된 단어는?
   a) muséum b) befóre c) transportátion
   d) ultímately e) democrátic

4. 다음에 해당되는 말은?

   Places offering sleeping accommodations for hire to travelers and transients.

   a) casino b) cloakroom c) dressing room
   d) hotel e) banquet room

5. 아래 빈칸에 맞는 단어를 찾아 문맥을 이으시오.
   He is in charge__________the front office.
   a) of b) for c) about
   d) at e) to

※ 빈칸에 알맞은 단어를 찾아 문맥을 이으시오.

6. How can I get_________touch with you?

a) in b) on c) to

d) with e) into

7. Bill was angry because his mother would not ________ him go to the movies.

a) permit b)let c) allow

d)get e) accept

8. 화법의 변화가 맞는 것은?

a) He said to me, "Will you help me?" He told me if I would help him.

b) He said, "I saw this man." He said that he saw that man.

c) He said to me, "I need a bike, but he had no money to buy one." He said me that he needed a bike, but he had no money to buy one.

d) He said to Mary, "You look happy." He told Mary that you looked happy.

e) I'm sorry I was not happy. I wish I were happy.

9. 어법에 맞는 것은?

I don't think Mary will stay here long, ____________?

a) doesn't she b) will she c) won't she

d) did she e) didn't she

10. 각 쌍의 의미가 서로 같지 않은 것은?

a) He left Korea never to return.
He left Korea for good.

b) I warned them not to go out.
I warned them that they should not go out.

c) You will do well to speak more slowly.

You will do well if you speak more slowly.

d) He pushed the door open for her to enter.
He pushed the door open that she might not enter.

e) Would you mind if I smoke here?
Would you mind my smoking here?

11. 어법에 맞지 않는 문장은?

a) A burglar robbed a customer of his money last night.

b) They laid the tools in the kitchen last night.

c) I envy you your fine voice.

d) Mr. Smith married with Elizabeth.

※ 서로의 대화가 문맥에 맞는 것은?(12-13)

12. A : There is water all over the bathroom floor.
B : Oh, I'm sorry I'll send the _______ up right.

a) room maid b) bell boy c) door man

c) plumber e) front clerk

13. A : I cleaned your room this morning.
B : It's very kind _____ you to do so.

a) for b) of c) with

d) about e) to

14. 뜻풀이가 잘못된 것은?

a) ginger:생강 b) garlic:마늘 c) vinegar:식초

d) mustard:후추 e) lettuce:상추

15. ___________ is a formal document issued by a competent officer of a country to a citizen of the country and usually necessary for exit from and reentry into the country, that certifies to the identity and citizenship of the bearer.

a) Passport

b) Visa

c) Government formalities
d) Vaccination certificate
e) 1-20 Form

16. __________ is issued to aliens who pass through Korea in order to go to a third country from their own, or vice versa, and the period of stay is for 15 days.
a) Tourist visa b) Transit visa c) Entry visa
d) SOFA visa e) Multiple visa

17. 다음 약자의 풀이가 잘못된 것은?
a) W.T.O. : World Tourism Organization
b) E.T.D. : the estimated time of departure
c) ASTA : American Society of Travel Agents
d) C.I.Q. : Customs, Immigration and Questionnaire
e) P.A.T.A. : Pacific Asia Travel Association

18. 영문의 해석이 맞지 않는 것은?
a) The line is dead. (전화 불통이야)
b) You are wanted on the phone. (전화왔어요)
c) Who am I speaking with? (누구를 대드릴까요?)
d) There is no one here by that name. (그런 사람 없어요)
e) I'm sorry to have kept you waiting so long. (오랫동안 기다리게 해서 죄송합니다.)

19. 술을 한잔 권할 때 쓰는 말로 적절한 것은?
Would you (　　) a glass of wine?
a) care about b) care for
c) have the care of d) give care to e) take

20. "Why don't you have another drink?"에서 another의 의미는?
a) different b) one more c) a lot of
d) plenty e) much

21. I'm looking forward to (   ) you in the near future. 위 문맥에 맞는 것은?
    a) seeing   b)see   c) have seen
    d) had seen   e) having been seen

※ 다음 밑줄 친 부분의 발음이 다른 셋과 같지 않은 것은?(22-23)

22. a) only   b) purpose   c) ago
    d) sew   e) know

23. a) certificate   b) declaration   c) communicate
    d) congratulate   e) immigrate

※ 다음 질문에 대한 답이 적합치 않은 것은?

24. How would you like your steak, sir?
    a) Medium, please.   b) Well-done, please.
    c) Rare, please.   d) Turned over, please.
    e) Medium rare, please.

※ 빈칸에 알맞은 것은?(25-31)

25. I don't want to _________ to the States.
    a) immigrate   b) apply   c) leave
    d) emigrate   e) start

26. Do you have any seat ___________?
    a) pleasures   b) preferences   c) prefers
    d) positions   e) preferring

27. ______ is the KAL check-in counter?
    a) Who   b) When   c) Where
    d) Why   e) What

28. She was deprived ________ all hope.

a) from b) of c) for
d) against e) to

29. A : Reservation desk, Miss Lee speaking. What can I help you, sir?

B : I'd like to ______ a reservation at your hotel.

a) ask b) reserve c) request
d) make e) arrange

30. What's the language ________ in Australia?

a) spoken b) speaking c) talked
d) told e) having talked

31. B : How would you like your Scotch?

A : Before supper I'd like to have a Scotch on the __________.

a) ice b) rocks c) cold water
d) mixed ice e) soda fountain

32. 식사 용어 중 철자가 모두 맞게 된 것은?

a) apetizer, entree, cashier, dessert
b) appetizer, entre, casher, desert
c) appetizer, entree, cashier, dessert
d) appetizer, entree, cashier, desert
e) apetizer, entre, cashier, dessert

33. 아래 영어의 올바른 해석은?

> Would you accept a collect call from Miss Rose Beston in New York?

a) New York의 Rose Beston양에게 수신인 요금부담 전화를 거시겠습니까?
b) New York의 Rose Beston에게서 오는 수신인 요금부담 전화를 받으시겠습니까?

c) New York의 Rose Beston에게 지명인 국제전화를 거시겠습니까?
d) New York의 Rose Beston에게 국제전화를 거시겠습니까?
e) New York의 Rose Beston이 요금부담하는 전화를 받으시겠어요?

34. Who is your __________ sponsor? **문맥에 맞는 것을 고르시오.**

a) financial b) finance c) financing
d) financer e) financier

35. 각 쌍의 문장 내용이 다른 것은?

a) The line is out of order. The line broke down.
b) Shall I have him call you when he comes in? Would you like him to call you when he gets back?
c) Could you speak up, please? Please speak a little louder.
d) The number doesn't ring a bell. The line is out of order so that I can't get through.
e) No one answered the phone. There was no answer.

36. A : B 간의 대화가 어색한 것은?

a) A : I'm sorry, but I broke your window.
B : That's all right.
b) A : I can't come to the meeting tomorrow.
B : That's right. You're going to New York, aren't you?
c) A : What time would you like to make it?
B : I'd like to fly to Singapore.
d) A : What is this regarding?
B : This is regarding our appointment.
e) A : I'm afraid I wear out my welcome.
B : Feel free to drop in and have a talk.

37. 각 문의 "make"의 용법이 어색한 문장은?

a) Did you make a reservation?
b) I'd like to make a long distance call to Pusan.
c) We made a bad connection.
d) I made an overseas call to New York last night.
e) I'll make him visit you, when he comes in.

38. 용어의 해설이 맞지 않는 것은?

a) table d'hôte: Infixed priced meal
b) á la carte: each food item on the menu is priced separately
c) suite : accommodations that include two rooms, one for sleeping and another for sitting, as well as a private bath.
d) tourism : all activities outside of home community except daily commuting to and from work
e) twin : hotel room having two single beds for use by two persons.

39. 어법이 옳다고 생각되는 것은?

a) Would you mind Robert's coming to the party?
b) Would you mind him to open the window?
c) Would you mind trading a seat with me?
d) Would you mind your opening the window?
e) Would you mind to come to the party this evening?

40. 다음 우리말이 잘못된 것은?

a) person-to-person call: 지명인 전화
b) station-to-station call: 대국전화
c) overseas call: 국제전화
d) long distance call: 장거리전화
e) collect call: 신청인 요금 부담전화

41. 영어의 풀이가 잘못된 것은?

a) guest-night: one night spent by one guest in a hotel or other accommodation
b) guided tour : unescorted sightseeing tour
c) domestic tour: use of tourism facilities within some legally bordered area, usually a nation, by the residents of that area
d) cultural tourism that focuses upon the rich past of a people or areas as preserved and portrayed in remains, historic sites, traditional architecture, and artifacts
e) total travel time: amount of time it actually takes to travel from one point to another, including all ground time along the way.

42. 빈칸에 가장 적절한 것은?

I would like a _______ for my headache.

a) pillow b) blanket c) quilt
d) pill e) vitamin

43. Show me your passport and ________ declaration forms.

a) costumes b) claims c) customs
d) check e) luggage

44. "오랫동안 기다리게 해서 죄송합니다."에 가장 적합한 표현은?

a) I'm sorry to have kept you waiting so long.
b) I'm sorry to keep you wait for a long time.
c) Excuse me, but may I take your time for a while?
d) Excuse me, but will you give me a little time?
e) I'm sorry, to make you waste your time so long.

45. A에 대한 대꾸로서 B에 대한 대답이 어법에 맞지 <u>않는</u> 것은?

a) A : He didn't say anything.
B : Neither did she.
b) A : They don't know Tom.
B : I don't, either.
c) A : I like apples so much.
B : Neither do I.
d) A : He went to the movies last night.
B : I did, too.
e) A : I was very upset when he didn't trust me.
B : So was I.

46. 어법에 맞지 <u>않는</u> 것은?

a) Every one of the windows was broken.
b) Everybody has their own book.
c) The baby drinks its milk.
d) All is not gold that glitters.
e) Time and tide wait for none.

47. 다음 A에 대한 응답으로 맞지 않는 것은?

A : How would you like your eggs, sir?
B : ______________________.

a) Turned over, please. b) Sunny side up, please.
c) Scrambled, please. d) Medium, please.
e) Poached, please.

48. 길을 물을 때 적합한 표현을 만드시오.
Excuse me, but show me ( ) the railroad station is.
a) where b) when c) how
d) what e) why

49. 빈칸에 가장 적합한 것을 찾아 문맥을 이으시오.
Please show me ( ) use this seat belt.
a) what b) how to c) where to
d) why to e) not to

50. 문맥에 맞는 표현을 고르시오.
I have no ( ) to stay at your hotel.
a) attention b) ckech-in c) intention
d) invention e) walks-in

※ 다음 빈칸에 알맞은 것은?

51. The front office is part of the __________.
a) front of the house b) reservation
c) room clerk d) registration card
e) back of the house

52. Please fill out the ___________?
a) information desk b) mezzanine
c) motel d) message box
e) registration card

53. The ________ will give you your room number.
a) waiter b) room clerk c) bartender
d) cashier e) chef

54. You can check in at the ________.
a) cloak room b)kitchen
c) registraiton desk d) suite e) station

55. Person who manages the bell service = ( )
a) baby-sitter b) skipper c) doorperson
d) bell captain e) VIP

56. Call a ___ ___ and ask for the price of a train ticket to Pusan.
a) general manager
b) chief engineer
c) food and beverage manager
d) reservation clerk
e) travel agent

57. We can take either a taxi or the ________ to the airport.
a) airport limousine b) motel c) reservation
d) stationery e) baby-sitter

58. She needs more ________ to finish her letter.
a) bookstore b) stationery c) doorman
d) drugstore e) front office

59. Vacancy = ( ).
a) message box b) hotel
c) unoccupied room d) nightclub e)lecture

60. Server of alcoholic beverages = ( ).
a) busboy b)cook c) hostess
d) bartender e) kitchen helper

61. busboy = (　　　　　).
    a) a light meal　　b) female greeter
    c) preparer of food　　d) server of wine
    e) cleaner of tables

62. The ________ is in charge of the banquet.
    a) banquet manager　　b) operator
    c) busboy　　d)cook
    e) information clerk

63. Since I don't have any money, I'll have to make a ________ to my parents.
    a) local call　　b) collect call
    c) long-distance call　　d) wake-up call
    e) person-to-person call

64. The hotel operator operates the ________.
    a) housekeeping　　b) front desk
    c) switchboard　　d) bar　　e) coffee shop

65. That hotel needs another ________ for its switchboard.
    a) chef　　b) cook　　c) waiter
    d) operator　　e) bookkeeper

66. They took the ________ to the 2nd floor.
    a) subway　　b) bus　　c) taxi
    d) train　　e) escalator

67. The grounds keeper mowed the ________.
    a) lawn　　b) room　　c) bar
    d) toilet　　e) escalator

68. Without an ________ this room would be very hot.
    a) occupier　　b) air conditioner　　c) observatory
    d) owner　　e) opener

69. "____________" was written over the door.

a) Lecture b) Advertisement c) Emergency Exit
d) Room Service e) Conference

70. The ___________ is next in line to the manager.

a) room maid b) bell captain c) room clerk
d) assistant manager e) cashier

71. When we prepare food at tableside, we are using ______________.

a) American Service b) Room Service c) Russian Service
d) Tray Service e) French Service

72. Items are priced individually on an ________ menu.

a) á la carte b) table d'hôte c) English
d) American e) Australian

73. The salt and pepper shakers go in the middle of the table in our ____________.

a) bar b) table setting c) cash register
d) table charge e) wine list

74. If a customer doesn't want to pay for a guest check with cash, he or she can use a _____________.

a) cash b)bank book c) credit card
d) cash e) map

75. Most restaurant employee wears a ___________.

a) coat b)cap c) tie
d) uniform e)hat

76. Do you have enough _________, pepper, and other condiments?

a) apple b) food c) silver ware
d) pineapple e) salt

77. There is more ______ on a busy day than on a slow day.

a) turnover b)VIP c) stationery

d) skipper e) room service

78. The __________ for a martini is an olive.

a) table setting b) garnish c) bartending

d) service e) decoration

79. Let's have a drink at a nearby ___________.

a) drug-store b) room c)bar

d) station e) store

80. The main part of a meal is known as the .

a) appetizer b) butcher c) check

d) entree e) convention

81. An ____________ is served before the entree.

a) orange b) officer

c) organization chart d) order e) appetizer

82. Use a ________ to weigh the ingredients for the bread.

a) scale b) shaker c) machine

d) powder e) mixer

83. The person who assists guests with their baggage, shows them to their rooms, and runs errands.

a) bus boy b) bellman c) dish washer

d) kitchen helper e) door man

84. The ___________ is presented to a customer at the end of a meal to indicate the cost of the meal.

a) menu b) wine list c) guest check

d) accounting e) D/C

∗ Fill in the blanks with the proper words from the lists.

1. masterkey	2. doorman	3. check-out time
4. bus boy	5. twin	6. double
7. dry goods	8. grand total	9. shift
10. aperitif	11. party	12. meal service

85. Today's (   ) begins at twelve noon.

86. Seat this (   ) at the corner table.

87. An (   ) is a drink that is served before dinner.

88. The day (   ) begins at nine a.m. and ends at five p.m.

89. A (   ) is a final total.

90. Sugar and flour are considered (   ).

91. A room with one large bed for two persons = (   ).

92. A room with two single beds for two persons. = (   ).

93. The person who cleans tables and pours water for customers in a restaurant = (   ).

94. The hour at which a guest must vacate a room = (   ).

95. The person who assists hotel guests in and out of vehicles in front of the hotel. = (   ).

96. a key that can open several different locks. = (   ).

97. I don't want to ________ to the states.

a) immigrate b) apply c) emigrate
d) leave e) intend

98. Have you ever ________ for a visa before?

a) asked b) denied c) wanted
d) applied e) returned

99. ________ was the first tour conductor.

a) Thomas Crook b)Thomas Kook
c) Tom Coke d)Thomas Smith
e) Thomas Cook

100. What is the WTO?

a) World Tourism Office
b) World Transport Office
c) World Travel Organization
d) World Tourism Organization
e) World Transport Organization

101. I would like a ________ for my head, please.

a) blanket b) pillow c) nap
d) board e) pill

102. ________ is the time difference between Seoul and New York?

a) When b) How c) What
d) Much e) Where

103. ________ does KAL flight 102 leave?

a) Why b) Wear c) Wind
d) When e) What

104. When is the next ________ flight?

a) collecting b) connecting c) correcting
d) transit e) changing

105. I'd like to make a _______ at the hotel.

a) reserve b) stay c)bed
d) reservation e) registration

106. I'm-leaving the hotel today. I'd like to ________.

a) confirm b) check in c) check up
d) check out e) change

107. Show me your passport and _______ declaration form, please.
a) counter b) costumes c) customs
d) check out e) change

108. What is your _____ of Korea?
a) expression b) thinking c) impression
d) convention e) conversaton

109. Can I ask a ______ of you?
a) flavor b) favorite c) favored
d) favor e) favors

110. _________ does it cost?
a) How many b) How often c) When
d) How much e) How expensive

111. What does EATA stand for?
a) East Asia Travel Agents
b) East Asia Tourism Association
c) East Asian Tour Association
d) East Asia Travel Association
e) East Afirca Test Association

112. Are you a ________ passenger?
a) transfer b) trnasmit c) transit
d) trouble e) transient

113. ________ is the KAL information desk?
a) When b) What c) Where
d) Wear e) Why

114. I have no __________ to stay in the states.
a) invention b) intention c) attention
d) immigrant e) emigrant

115. Have you ever __________ for a visa before?

a) apply　b) applies　c) applied
d) application　e) appled

116. hat is USTS?

a) United States Tour Service
b) United States Tourism Service
c) United States Travel Society
d) United States Tourism Society
e) United States Travel Service

117. When do we __________ in Seoul?

a) arrival　b) arrive　c) arrived
d) arrives　e) arriving

118. Who is your ________ sponsor?

a) finance　b) financial　c) financing
d) financer　e) financials

119. Do you have a __________ ?

a) reserve　b) reservations　c) reservation
d) reserved　e) reserving

120. __________ to the post office?

a) How do I go　b) What do get
c) How do I get　d) How do you want
e) How does I get

121. When is _________ time? I want to leave.

a) checking　b) checkers　c) check in
d) check-out　e) checker out

122. Would you care for something to _________ before dmner?

a) drank　b) drink　c) drunk
d) drinking　e) drinks

123. __________ is a beer?

a) How many b) How much c) How often
d) How costs e) How may

124. May I ________ to miss Kim, please?

a) spoke b) spoken c) speak
d) speaking e) speaker

125. ________ would you like to order?

a) How b) What c) Where
d) Why e) May

126. I want to make a ________ call.

a) correct b)connect c) collect
d) correcting e) collective

127. Excuse me, but __________ is the train station?

a) when b) where c) what
d) how e) why

128. __________ do you want to go today?

a) Where b) How c) Much
d) May e) Why

129. _________ there a subway station near here?

a) Was b) Will c)Is
d) Are e) Were

130. Where can I ________ a western restrurant?

a) found b) look c) finds
d) find e) founds

131. Welcome to this sightseeing ________.

a) travel b) tours c)tourism
d) tour e) touring

132. __________ you care for a cup of tea?
a) Could b) Should c) Would
d) What e) When

133. __________ do you graduate from school?
a) Will b) Where c) When
d) What e) Why

134. ________ are you going to buy? (무엇을 사렵니까?)
a) Why b) Will c) What
d) When e) Where

135. ________ long have you been sick?
a) Much b) Have c) How
d) Where e) When

136. What _________ you most about your trip to Japan?
a) expressed b) impress c) impressive
d) impressed e) expressed

137. I've just ________ in Seoul.
a) departed b) departure c) arrival
d) arrive e) arrived

138. Would you show me ________ use chopsticks?
a) when to b) have to c) how am
d) how to e) how are

139. What ______ your hobby?
a) was b) were c) are
d) is e) am

저자와의
합의하에
인지첩부
생략

관광서비스영어

2003년 2월 10일 초판 1쇄 발행
2021년 2월 20일 초판 12쇄 발행

지은이 이완형
펴낸이 진욱상
펴낸곳 백산출판사
교 정 편집부
본문디자인 편집부
표지디자인 오정은

등 록 1974년 1월 9일 제406-1974-000001호
주 소 경기도 파주시 회동길 370(백산빌딩 3층)
전 화 02-914-1621(代)
팩 스 031-955-9911
이메일 edit@ibaeksan.kr
홈페이지 www.ibaeksan.kr

ISBN 89-7739-508-9 93740
값 15,000원